SpringerBriefs in Criminology

SpringerBriefs in Criminology present concise summaries of cutting edge research across the fields of Criminology and Criminal Justice. It publishes small but impactful volumes of between 50-125 pages, with a clearly defined focus. The series covers a broad range of Criminology research from experimental design and methods, to brief reports and regional studies, to policy-related applications.

The scope of the series spans the whole field of Criminology and Criminal Justice, with an aim to be on the leading edge and continue to advance research. The series will be international and cross-disciplinary, including a broad array of topics, including juvenile delinquency, policing, crime prevention, terrorism research, crime and place, quantitative methods, experimental research in criminology, research design and analysis, forensic science, crime prevention, victimology, criminal justice systems, psychology of law, and explanations for criminal behavior.

SpringerBriefs in Criminology will be of interest to a broad range of researchers and practitioners working in Criminology and Criminal Justice Research and in related academic fields such as Sociology, Psychology, Public Health, Economics and Political Science.

Marcelo F. Aebi • Fernando Miró-Llinares
Stefano Caneppele
Editors

Understanding Crime Trends in a Hybrid Society

The Digital Drift

Editors
Marcelo F. Aebi
School of Criminal Sciences
Faculty of Law, Criminal Sciences and
Public Administration
University of Lausanne
Lausanne, Switzerland

Fernando Miró-Llinares
Crimina Center
University Miguel Hernández of Elche
Elche, Spain

Stefano Caneppele
School of Criminal Sciences
Faculty of Law, Criminal Sciences and
Public Administration
University of Lausanne
Lausanne, Switzerland

ISSN 2192-8533   ISSN 2192-8541   (electronic)
SpringerBriefs in Criminology
ISBN 978-3-031-72386-5   ISBN 978-3-031-72387-2   (eBook)
https://doi.org/10.1007/978-3-031-72387-2

This book is an open access publication.

© The Editor(s) (if applicable) and The Author(s) 2025
Open Access This book is licensed under the terms of the Creative Commons Attribution 4.0 International License (http://creativecommons.org/licenses/by/4.0/), which permits use, sharing, adaptation, distribution and reproduction in any medium or format, as long as you give appropriate credit to the original author(s) and the source, provide a link to the Creative Commons license and indicate if changes were made.
The images or other third party material in this book are included in the book's Creative Commons license, unless indicated otherwise in a credit line to the material. If material is not included in the book's Creative Commons license and your intended use is not permitted by statutory regulation or exceeds the permitted use, you will need to obtain permission directly from the copyright holder.
The use of general descriptive names, registered names, trademarks, service marks, etc. in this publication does not imply, even in the absence of a specific statement, that such names are exempt from the relevant protective laws and regulations and therefore free for general use.
The publisher, the authors and the editors are safe to assume that the advice and information in this book are believed to be true and accurate at the date of publication. Neither the publisher nor the authors or the editors give a warranty, expressed or implied, with respect to the material contained herein or for any errors or omissions that may have been made. The publisher remains neutral with regard to jurisdictional claims in published maps and institutional affiliations.

This Springer imprint is published by the registered company Springer Nature Switzerland AG
The registered company address is: Gewerbestrasse 11, 6330 Cham, Switzerland

If disposing of this product, please recycle the paper.

Acknowledgements

We would like to express our gratitude to Lucas Tosi Rodriguez for his excellent work in formatting and preparing this book for publication. His dedication has been essential for this project. Thank you, Lucas, for your outstanding support. We also acknowledge the use of ChatGPT and Claude as tools for text editing and refinement during the manuscript preparation. While ChatGPT and Claude played a role in enhancing the language and sentence structure, all ideas, analyses, and perspectives presented in this book are the original contributions of the authors. Fernando Miró-Llinares states that his contribution was made possible thanks to the grant Programa Prometeo 2023- CIPROM/2022/33 offered by the Generalitat Valenciana.

Introduction: The Digital Transformation of Crime: Understanding Trends and Patterns in Our Hybrid Society

The digital revolution of the past few decades has profoundly transformed society, creating what can be termed a "hybrid society" where physical and digital spaces increasingly interweave and overlap in our daily lives. This fundamental transformation has reshaped how we communicate, work, and structure our routines, blurring traditional boundaries between online and offline activities. As our world becomes increasingly interconnected and digitalized, the hybrid nature of modern society has also transformed patterns of criminal behavior. New forms of crime have emerged in cyberspace, while traditional offline crimes have evolved or declined. Understanding these complex changes in criminal activity—which often traverse both physical and digital domains—presents both challenges and opportunities for criminologists, law enforcement, and policymakers.

This book explores the multifaceted relationship between digitalization and crime trends, examining how the digital transformation of society has influenced patterns of criminal behavior, victimization, and law enforcement responses. The volume progresses from broad theoretical foundations through empirical analyses to methodological considerations, offering a comprehensive examination of how digitalization has affected crime patterns over time.

The first chapter establishes the historical and philosophical foundations of criminology's progressive ethos, providing context for understanding how the field approaches technological change and its effects on crime. This examination of criminology's intellectual roots helps frame the subsequent discussion of digital transformation and crime trends.

The second chapter presents a systematic review of the scholarly debate surrounding the concept of an "international crime drop" since the 1990s. Through analysis of four distinct interpretative narratives, it shows that researchers have attempted to explain observed declines in certain types of offline crime across multiple countries, highlighting the complex relationship between technological change and criminal behavior.

The third chapter develops a theoretical framework for understanding how digitalization influences social change and crime trends. Through a literature review, it proposes a conjecture about the mechanisms through which digital transformation affects criminal behavior and victimization patterns, considering both direct and indirect effects of technological change.

The fourth chapter presents empirical evidence for the "digital leisure hypothesis," examining how increased engagement with digital entertainment, particularly among youth, has contributed to shifts in criminal opportunities. This chapter provides concrete data supporting the theoretical frameworks developed earlier in the volume while also exploring how the COVID-19 pandemic has accelerated existing trends in digital behavior and crime patterns.

The fifth chapter offers a scoping review of cybercrime research methods and measurement approaches, examining how researchers have studied different types of cybercrime and the methodological challenges they face. This chapter provides insights into the strengths and limitations of current research methods and the challenges of measuring crime in the digital age.

Together, these chapters address several key questions at the intersection of technology and criminology:

- How has the rise of digital technology affected trends in different types of crime?
- What new forms of criminal activity have emerged in the digital age?
- How can cybercrime be effectively measured and analyzed given the limitations of traditional crime statistics?
- What criminological theories and frameworks are most useful for explaining crime in the digital era?
- How should law enforcement and criminal justice systems adapt to address the challenges of cybercrime?

The volume also addresses crucial methodological questions about how cybercrime can be effectively studied and measured:

- What approaches have researchers used to study different types of cybercrime?
- What are the main methodological challenges in measuring cybercrime?
- How can official statistics be adapted to better capture cybercrime?
- What are the strengths and limitations of current research methods?

By bringing together historical analysis, theoretical development, empirical research, and methodological considerations, this volume offers a comprehensive examination of how technological change is reshaping criminal activity and our responses to it. The insights presented here have relevant implications for criminological theory, crime prevention strategies, and criminal justice policy in an increasingly digital world.

As our hybrid society continues to evolve in the digital age, criminology progresses with it. This book contributes to that ongoing effort by highlighting the complex and dynamic relationship between technology and crime in the twenty-first century. Through an analysis of both historical trends and contemporary data, the chapters that follow offer readers a nuanced understanding of crime patterns in our hybrid physical-digital world.

Lausanne, Switzerland	Marcelo F. Aebi
Elche, Spain	Fernando Miró-Llinares
Lausanne, Switzerland	Stefano Caneppele
January 2025	

Contents

1	**The Roots and Ramifications of Criminology's Progressive Ethos: Navigating Theory, Practice, and Politics**	1
	Marcelo F. Aebi	
	The Emperor's New Clothes or Wisdom in Humor	1
	Progress and the Enlightenment	3
	The Philosophical Discourse on Progress	3
	The Philosophical Discourse on Scientific Progress	4
	The Enlightenment and Politics	5
	The Enlightenment and the Rise of the Social Sciences	6
	The Progressive Ethos of Criminology	7
	The Debate Between Reform-Oriented and Problem-Solving Criminologists	10
	Challenges and Limitations of the Progressive Ethos in Criminology: The Offline Crime Drop in the United States as a Case Study	11
	Conclusion	13
	References	14
2	**A Narrative Review of the Debate on the So-Called International Crime Drop**	17
	Marcelo F. Aebi	
	The Rise of a Concept: The International Crime Drop	17
	The American Context	17
	Expansion to Other Countries	18
	Complexities and Variations	18
	Challenges to the Concept	18
	A Timeline of the Debate on the International Crime Drop	19
	1997–1998: The Initial Recognition	19
	1998: Political Recognition	19
	1999: International Perspectives Emerge	20
	2000: Expanding the Discourse	20

	2004: Cross-National Studies and Eastern European Perspectives.	21
	2005: Comprehensive Analysis of Western Countries	21
	2007: Victimization Perspective	21
	2010: Challenging the Universality	21
	2012: New Directions in Research	22
	2014: Comprehensive Review and Theoretical Developments.	22
	2018: Bringing Crime Trends Back into Criminology	22
The All-American Narratives		23
The Lausanne School Narrative		24
	Crime Trends in Europe from 1990 to 1996: How Europe Illustrates the Limits of the American Experience	25
	Crime Trends in Western Europe from 1990 to 2000	26
	Is There a Crime Drop in Western Europe?	27
	Conviction Statistics as an Indicator of Crime Trends	28
	Crime Trends in Western Europe, 1990–2007	28
	Is There a Relationship Between Imprisonment and Crime in Western Europe?	29
	The Persistence of Lifestyles: Rates and Correlates of Homicide in Western Europe from 1960 to 2010	29
	Crime Drop or Police Recording Flop? On the Relationship Between the Decrease of Offline Crime and the Increase of Online and Hybrid Crimes	30
	Comparative Criminology in the Digital Society	31
	Summary of the Contribution of the Lausanne School.	31
The *Crime and Justice* Narrative		32
	Crime and Punishment in Western Countries, 1980–1999	33
	Why Crime Rates Are Falling Throughout the Western World	34
The Security Hypothesis Narrative		36
Discussion and Conclusion		38
References		40
3	**Digitalization, Social Change, and Crime Trends: A Literature Review to Build a Conjecture**	**45**
	Fernando Miró-Llinares and Marcelo F. Aebi	
	What Slow and Abrupt Changes Can Have in Common	45
	The Role of Technology, Opportunity, and Lifestyles Changes on Crime Trends	48
	The Disputed, But Always Alive, Hypothesis of a Relationship Between Digitalization and the Offline Crime Drop (and Its Misunderstandings)	51
	An Overview of Studies on the Link Between Digitalization and the Offline Crime Drop	51
	Beyond Misunderstandings: On the "Heart," Chronology, and Scope of the Conjecture	57

	The Literature on Youth Crime Trends (Beyond the Crime Drop), a New Clue to the Conjecture	63
	Pointing at the Elephant in the Room	67
	References	69
4	**Crime Opportunities, Lockdowns, and Online Video Games: The Digital Leisure Hypothesis (and More on the Impact of Digitalization on Crime Trends)**	77
	Fernando Miró-Llinares	
	On Lockdown and Its Consequences	77
	One Digital Revolution, One Crime Trend, One Micro Mechanism, or Many of Them? Analytical Decomposition of the Bases of the Conjecture	80
	The Conjecture and Its Early Developments: On the Impact on Crime Trends Since 1990	87
	The Digital Leisure Hypothesis: The Impact of the Change in the Routines of Young People Due to Digital Leisure in the So-Called "Crime Drop"	88
	Building the New Digital Opportunities Hypothesis: About the Hidden But Real Impact on Trends in the Emergence of New Media to Perpetrate Internet Crime	93
	A New Hypothesis for the Future: Covid-19 Crisis, the Acceleration of Digitalization and Future Crime Trends	96
	References	96
5	**Observing, Measuring, and Researching Cybercrime: A Scoping Review of Systematic Reviews Since 2010s**	101
	Stefano Caneppele	
	Introduction	101
	On the Challenges in Measuring (Cyber)crime(s) and Their Trends	102
	To Be, or Not to Be (Cybercrime), That Is the Question	105
	Scoping the Empirical Research on Cybercrime	108
	Which Cybercrimes Have Been More Investigated?	110
	Which Criminological and Non-criminological Theories Have Been More Tested?	112
	Which Types of Data and Analytical Method Have Been Used?	114
	What Are the Findings of Criminological and Non-criminological Research?	116
	Conclusion: The Strain of Measuring Cybercrime in the Information Age	122
	References	123

Epilogue: The Evolution of Crime in Our Hybrid Society: Looking Back, Looking Forward, and Looking More Carefully 129

Index 131

About the Editors

Marcelo F. Aebi, Ph.D., is a Full Professor of Criminology at the University of Lausanne, Switzerland. He is a consultant expert for the Council of Europe, Head of the European Sourcebook Group, and Executive Secretary of the European Society of Criminology. Specializing in comparative criminology and crime indicators, he has a prolific output of scientific publications in several languages. For details, see marceloaebi.com.

Fernando Miró-Llinares, Ph.D., is a Full Professor of Criminal Law and Criminology at the Miguel Hernández University of Elche (Spain) and Head of the CRÍMINA Research Centre for the Study and Prevention of Crime at the same university. He is also Coordinator of the Summer School and a former member of the Executive Board of the European Society of Criminology. His research areas include cybercrime, environmental criminology, artificial intelligence, fake news, and online radicalization, among others.

Stefano Caneppele, Ph.D., is a Full Professor of Criminology and Deputy Director at the School of Criminal Sciences of the University of Lausanne, Switzerland. He is a consultant expert for the Council of Europe and co-chairs the European Society of Criminology Working Group on Crime, Criminal Justice, and the COVID-19 Pandemic. His main research areas include crime prevention, cybercrime, economic crime, and organized crime.

Chapter 1
The Roots and Ramifications of Criminology's Progressive Ethos: Navigating Theory, Practice, and Politics

Marcelo F. Aebi

> *The idea of progress, conceived as the increasing sophistication of knowledge and the improving quality of life, has been the driving force of Western civilization for at least three hundred years.*
>
> "Progress" (Scott & Marshall, 2015)

The Emperor's New Clothes or Wisdom in Humor

For a reason that is not relevant here, in May 2002, while still a young lecturer, I was invited to give a plenary talk at the biannual conference of the Association of French-Speaking Criminologist (AICLF) in Liège, Belgium. During one of the meals, I had the good fortune of sharing the table with Christian Debuyst and Maurice Cusson. In 1996, Debuyst had received the AICLF Beaumont-Tocqueville Award, which honors a lifetime contribution to criminological research and criminal policy reform, and Cusson would receive it in 2010. They had known each other for many years, and when I joined them at the table, they were already in high spirits, laughing heartily. Debuyst then shared the source of their amusement. It was something that happened several years ago, when they were both attending a meeting of criminologists—probably labeled as a meeting of sociologists of deviance, as it was typical in France in those days—in a very well-known French university. There, at the beginning of his plenary talk, Maurice stated: "*Parce que nous, les hommes de droite...*" (because we, right-wing men...). You should have seen the faces of the audience, Marcelo, said Christian; there was a sudden, tense silence and

---

M. F. Aebi (✉)
School of Criminal Sciences, Faculty of Law, Criminal Sciences and Public Administration, University of Lausanne, Lausanne, Switzerland
e-mail: marcelo.aebi@unil.ch

a moment of incredulity. Those who did not know Maurice were wondering: Is he joking? Should we leave the room?

The three of us burst into laughter, celebrating Maurice Cusson's audacity, his flair for provocation, and his ability to scandalize the self-righteous academics. Only a couple of years later, when I began reflecting on my unconscious preference for certain types of explanations and realized that much of the debate about the crime drop in the United States was ideological—with one side arguing that nothing good can come from the state in a free-market society and the other asserting that broken windows and hot spots policing effectively played a role—did I fully appreciate how this anecdote underscores a critical issue in academic and scientific communities. I became aware of how much I took for granted that we, social scientists, perceived ourselves as a community of progressive people and how this affected my search for objectivity when thinking about crime.

A few years later, Cusson's sarcastic humor had almost been banned from academia, especially in the United States.[1] Not only can you seldom joke about conservatism, but you can also easily be labeled as conservative if you do not share a specific *Weltanschauung*, and perhaps even face exclusion for conducting research that does not fit within that worldview. This is particularly troubling in the realm of science, where progress relies on open, inclusive, and respectful discourse. In 2021, Noam Chomsky expressed significant concerns about cancel culture, particularly its potential to stifle open debate and free speech. He worries that cancel culture could become deeply entrenched in public life, drawing parallels to the influence of French structuralist theory, which he critiques as elitist and overly academic (Paradox Politics, 2021). Chomsky is one of the well-known intellectuals who cosigned the "Letter on Justice and Open Debate" published in Harper's Magazine (2020). The letter warned against the growing intolerance of opposing views and the tendency for public shaming and ostracism, arguing that the free exchange of information and ideas is essential for a liberal society and democratic participation. The author of this chapter fully subscribes to this sentiment, and it is difficult to express these concerns better. That is why this chapter is not about cancel culture.

Instead, this chapter focuses on the origins of criminology's progressive ethos, its impact on the development of criminological scientific knowledge, and how this ethos has evolved in ways that some view as contradictory, but can be seen as complementary. The theme of international crime trends in the 1990s and 2000s, which serves as the backbone of this book, is used as a case example. The chapter begins by exploring the roots of the progressive ethos in the Enlightenment, discussing the philosophical discourse on progress and scientific progress. It then examines the Enlightenment's influence on politics and the rise of the social sciences, providing context for the development of criminology as a progressive discipline. The chapter goes on to analyze the progressive ethos in criminology, discussing various theories

---

[1] Maurice Cusson, today an emeritus professor, gave me his blessing to share this souvenir, mentioning that "at the time I couldn't help but provoke and that made people laugh. Nowadays, I would probably cause a scandal" (Cusson, personal communication, 11 June 2024, translated from French by me).

that aim to change individuals, societies, the criminal justice system, or the environment by addressing different causes of crime. This leads us to a critical juncture in the 1970s, with the emergence of two distinct approaches: reform-oriented criminology, exemplified by Marxist critical criminology and its derivates, and problem-solving criminology, exemplified by opportunity-based theories, also known as the situational approach, and their practical application through situational crime prevention. The chapter then delves into the debate between these two perspectives, highlighting the critiques and responses from each side. It also presents a case study of the debate surrounding the crime drop in the United States to illustrate the challenges and limitations of a reform-oriented progressive ethos in criminology. The chapter concludes by summarizing the main arguments, synthesizing the key points, and reflecting on the broader implications of the progressive ethos in criminology for the field's future direction and its role in promoting positive change, that is to say *progress*, in society.

Progress and the Enlightenment

The reasoning in this chapter is built upon several premises concerning scientific and general progress, which are closely associated with the European Enlightenment of the eighteenth century and its enduring influence. These premises are not presented as self-evident axioms, as such an approach would be considered presumptuous. Additionally, supporting these premises solely through personal analysis would raise concerns regarding objectivity. Therefore, these arguments are grounded in the conceptualizations presented by Tam and Meek Lange (2024) and Niiniluoto (2024) in *The Stanford Encyclopedia of Philosophy*, which will be followed in the next two sections.

The Philosophical Discourse on Progress

The philosophical discourse on progress, both moral and political, first gained prominence during the Age of Enlightenment (Tam & Meek Lange, 2024). This intellectual and political movement was grounded in the works of the French philosophers of the mid-eighteenth century, namely, Voltaire, D'Alembert, Diderot, and Montesquieu (Bristow, 2024). According to Tam and Meek Lange (2024), this period introduced the idea of history as progressive, countering the belief that it is merely a sequence of random events with no specific direction. Enlightenment thinkers viewed history as having a tendency toward freedom. This perspective is commonly associated with philosophers of the eighteenth and nineteenth century like Kant, Hegel, and Marx, who had differing views on the nature and conditions of historical progress but shared the Enlightenment's optimistic belief in the upward development of humanity. Their view was significantly influenced by the rise of modern science, which will be discussed in the next section. However, in the twentieth century, the maturation of evolutionary sciences challenged the Enlightenment view of progress and contributed to its decline. Always according to Tam and Meek Lange (2024), the optimism of the Enlightenment was replaced by a climate of despair, especially in light of world wars, colonial conquests, and environmental degradation. New intellectual traditions, such as critical theory, moral relativism, postcolonialism, and postmodernism, emerged to critique the metaphysical, epistemological, and empirical assumptions of the Enlightenment view of progress. These traditions highlighted the normative risks and presented an alternative picture of history that is often contingent, if not tragic, leading to an uncertain outlook on the future (Tam & Meek Lange, 2024).

The Philosophical Discourse on Scientific Progress

Niiniluoto (2024) states that science is often distinguished from other domains of human culture by its progressive nature, characterized by clear standards for identifying improvements and advances. According to Niiniluoto (2024), during the Enlightenment, the idea that the acquisition and systematization of positive knowledge are uniquely cumulative and progressive in science was pivotal. Classical empiricists like Francis Bacon and rationalists such as René Descartes argued that proper methods of inquiry ensure the discovery and justification of new truths. This optimism about the progressive nature of science was integral to the Enlightenment's belief in societal progress, as articulated in Auguste Comte's positivism. This period saw a strong connection between scientific advancements and societal improvement, supported by influential trends such as the romantic vision of organic growth, Hegel's dynamic historical change, and Charles Darwin's theory of evolution. However, in the twentieth century, this view was significantly challenged. Always according to Niiniluoto (2024), philosophers of science began to scrutinize the idea that science progresses simply by accumulating new truths. Key works such as Karl Popper's *The Logic of Scientific Discovery* (1959), Thomas Kuhn's *The Structure of Scientific Revolutions* (1970/1962), and Larry Laudan's *Progress and Its Problems* (1977) highlighted that scientific progress is not merely cumulative. They introduced the notion that scientific theories undergo paradigm shifts and revolutions, wherein older theories are replaced or reinterpreted rather than simply built upon. This shift in understanding marked a decline in the Enlightenment's optimistic view of continuous scientific progress. Instead, newer philosophical traditions began to emphasize the discontinuous and sometimes revolutionary nature of scientific change, leading to a more nuanced and less linear conception of scientific progress (Niiniluoto, 2024).

The Enlightenment and Politics

Initially rooted in the scientific revolution and the rise of modern science, which championed reason, empirical evidence, and the questioning of traditional dogma, the Enlightenment's scientific branch laid the groundwork for a new understanding of the world.[2] This scientific ethos naturally extended into the political sphere, where Enlightenment thinkers applied rational principles to criticize and reform societal structures. As mentioned above, they viewed history as progressive and this progression was toward freedom.

Enlightenment philosophers, such as Locke, Montesquieu, Rousseau, and Voltaire, argued that individuals possess natural rights that are inherent and inalienable, in the sense that they are derived from natural law rather than granted by governments. They advocated for the freedom of speech, religion, and the press, as well as freedom from oppressive governments and separation of powers. They also promoted the idea of equality before the law, considering that all individuals should have equal rights and opportunities. The ideas of Enlightenment philosophers directly influenced the French Revolution, particularly in the Declaration of the Rights of Man and of the Citizen, the American Revolution, and the drafting of the Declaration of Independence, as well as the independence movements across the Americas, and even laid the groundwork for modern human rights movements and documents, such as the Universal Declaration of Human Rights adopted by the United Nations in 1948.

In sum, the Enlightenment thinkers challenged the traditional power structures and this romantic idea of the intellectual individual against the state has fashioned the way in which some intellectuals self-perceive themselves and are perceived by others. These intellectuals can be seen as reform-oriented progressives as they want to radically change the established order.

The trouble is that the political order installed by the French revolution turned into the Reign of Terror, in which roughly 300,000 suspects were arrested, 17,000 were officially executed, and probably 10,000 died in prison or without trial, all suspected of being enemies of the Revolution.[3] This French Revolutionary Terror led to the rise of what became known as conservatism, represented by Burke and his preference for England's revolution of 1688 that proposed "a return to an alleged *status quo* prior to monarchical absolutism, as opposed to an overturning of traditional institutions in accord with a rational plan" (Hamilton, 2020). Revolutions conducted in the name of Marxists ideas also had a "rational plan" and systematically led to authoritarian regimes. This is precisely why there is another group of intellectuals that oppose reforms in the form of revolutions and promote gradual improvements usually based on practice (Hamilton, 2020). Even if these intellectu-

---

[2] For a general introduction to the Enlightenment, see Bristow (2024). For its influence today, see Pinker (2018).

[3] Britannica, T. Editors of Encyclopaedia (2024, January 27). *Reign of Terror. Encyclopedia Britannica.* https://www.britannica.com/event/Reign-of-Terror

als search to improve the well-being of humanity and could therefore be seen as progressives, they are often defined as conservatives. This political dimension of the Enlightenment should help us understand its impact on the social sciences.

The Enlightenment and the Rise of the Social Sciences

When discussing the rise of modern science as one of the driving forces behind the Enlightenment, the focus is primarily on the natural sciences, such as physics, chemistry, biology, and astronomy. These disciplines are closely linked to the Industrial Revolution, which began in the latter half of the eighteenth century. Nevertheless, the humanitarian component of the Enlightenment laid the ground for the development of the humanities and the social sciences. That is to say that the rise of the natural sciences is one of the causes of the Enlightenment, which in turn is one of the causes of the rise of the humanities and the social sciences.

In that perspective, Auguste Comte's positivism epitomizes the cumulative view of science, suggesting that knowledge progresses to the point where it can predict societal events (Comte, 1830 to 1842). Comte initially envisioned naming sociology "social physics," a term preempted by Adolphe Quetelet (1835). Consequently, Comte coined the term sociology, which can be seen as the precursor to contemporary criminology. Both fields, being products of the Enlightenment, are hence progressive in nature. Comte also coined the term "positivism," inspired by the expression "positive science," which emerged in the eighteenth century. Positivism refers to a method of knowledge production that rejects all metaphysical a priori assumptions and focuses on the observation of "positive" facts. In that context, "positive" refers to concrete experiences, to what can be observed, to the objective reality. This view is seen today as extremely optimistic toward what can be achieved through science, but Comte belongs to another era. As a reminder, it was also in the eighteenth century that the term optimism was coined and was immediately popularized by Voltaire in his book *Candide, ou l'Optimisme* published in 1759.

We have seen above that such optimism was replaced after the Second World War by a pessimistic view of progress that led to the development of critical theories, and he have also seen that contemporary philosophers of science developed a nonlinear view of progress and scientific change (Niiniluoto, 2024; Tam & Meek Lange, 2024). In criminology, in the 1960s and 1970s, this led to two different traditions. One corresponds to a Marxist tradition that has evolved, at least partially, toward postmodernist positions; the other one follows a problem-solving tradition and is characterized by opportunity-based theories.

The rise of Marxist critical criminology in the 1970s marked a significant shift in criminological thought. This approach sought to radically transform society by challenging the capitalist system that was seen as the root cause of crime and inequality. Marxist critical criminologists argued that the criminal justice system served to maintain the power of the ruling class and that true justice could only be achieved through a socialist revolution.[4] In the framework of this work, one can say that for them the aim of progress is to restructure the economic system to create a more just and equitable society. They do not want to save the world but to change it. In this context, they can be seen as reform-oriented progressives.

In contrast, opportunity-based theories, which emerged around the same time, took a more pragmatic and scientific approach that led them to develop what is known as situational crime prevention. Situational criminologists were influenced by the views of Popper (1957), Kuhn (1962, 1970), and Laudan (1977) on problem-solving. For instance, Laudan argued that science should focus on solving specific empirical problems rather than pursuing abstract theoretical goals. In a similar vein, situational criminologists seek to identify and solve the concrete problems that contribute to crime rather than pursuing grand theories of social transformation. They focus on identifying and changing the specific situations and environments that create opportunities for crime, emphasizing the importance of empirical research and practical interventions. Reducing crime will reduce fear of crime and improve the general well-being of the population. In this context, they can be seen as problem-solving progressives.

In practice, criminologist fully engaged in one or another of these contemporary approaches tend to have little mercy for those involved in the opposite one. Hence, reform-oriented criminologists often accuse problem-solving criminologists of doing "administrative criminology" while the latter label the former as "academic criminologists."

Despite significant differences between these approaches, both can be viewed as reflecting the enduring influence of the Enlightenment idea of progress within criminology. Reform-oriented criminologists aim to achieve progress through radical political change, whereas situational criminologists focus on incremental, evidence-based improvements in crime prevention. From this perspective, it can be concluded that the idea of progress continues to play a central role in criminology, even as the field has become increasingly fragmented and specialized.

The Progressive Ethos of Criminology

The Enlightenment's emphasis on individual rights and equality before the law had a significant impact on the development of early criminological thought. Philosophers such as Cesare Beccaria and Jeremy Bentham, who are often considered the founders of classical criminology, were heavily influenced by Enlightenment ideas (Newman, 1997).

Beccaria, in his seminal work *On Crimes and Punishments* (1764), argued for a more humane and rational approach to criminal justice. He advocated for the abolition of torture and the death penalty except under very restricted circumstances,

---

[4] See Quinney (1974, 1979), Spitzer (1975), and Taylor et al. (1973).

while proposing that punishments should be proportional to the crime committed. Beccaria's ideas were rooted in the Enlightenment's belief in individual rights and the social contract, which held that individuals surrender some of their freedoms to the state in exchange for protection of their remaining rights.

Similarly, Bentham, who developed the theory of utilitarianism, argued that the purpose of the criminal justice system should be to maximize happiness and minimize pain for the greatest number of people. He believed that punishments should serve as a deterrent to crime but should not be excessive or cruel. Bentham's ideas, like Beccaria's, were grounded in the Enlightenment's emphasis on reason, individual rights, and the social contract.

The influence of the Enlightenment on classical criminology laid the foundation for the progressive ethos in the field. By emphasizing the importance of individual rights, equality before the law, and the need for a more humane and rational approach to criminal justice, classical criminologists set the stage for future developments in the field that aimed to understand and address the causes of crime.

In this context, one can argue that the fundamental belief system driving criminological research and theory is the notion that humankind can progress, meaning that humans can change and move forward toward gradual betterment.[5] This progressive perspective manifests in various ways, contributing to the development of diverse criminological theories aimed at changing individuals, societies, the criminal justice system, or the environment. Their common goal is to understand the root causes of criminal behavior and propose interventions that reduce crime and enhance social well-being.

Some theories propose individual-level changes. For example, psychological approaches focus on individual psychological traits and childhood experiences. Their approaches include counseling, behavior modification programs, and rehabilitation efforts aimed at addressing underlying psychological issues. Similarly, biological approaches suggests that genetic and physiological factors contribute to criminal behavior. Their interventions include medical treatments, therapy, and programs addressing mental health issues. Deterrence theory, which is the basis of modern criminal codes, emphasizes that individuals make rational decisions based on a cost-benefit analysis. Consequently, its policies focus on deterrence through stricter laws and harsher punishments to discourage criminal behavior. Similarly, social learning theory proposes that individuals learn criminal behavior from their environment, including family, peers, and the media. Its interventions aim at promoting positive role models, reinforcing prosocial behavior, and providing educational and vocational training.

Other theories propose societal-level changes. For example, social disorganization theory attributes crime to the breakdown of community institutions and social norms. Its interventions include community development programs, improving

---

[5] According to the online Merriam-Webster dictionary, "a forward or onward movement (as to an objective of to a goal): advance" and "gradual betterment" are the second and third meaning of the noun "progress," while, logically, the verb means "to move forward: proceed" and "to develop a higher, better, or more advanced stage."

neighborhood infrastructure, and fostering community cohesion. Strain theory argues that societal pressure to achieve cultural goals, like wealth, can lead to crime when individuals lack legitimate means. Its policies focus on reducing inequality and providing opportunities through education, employment, and social services. Conflict theory, including Marxist perspectives, views crime as a result of social and economic inequality and power imbalances. Its policies advocate for systemic changes to address inequality, such as redistributive justice, fairer economic policies, and reforms to the criminal justice system.

Labeling theory concentrates on the ways in which the criminal law system itself contributes to the crime problem. It argues that the process of labeling individuals as criminals, through arrest, prosecution, and imprisonment, can actually reinforce criminal behavior and create a self-fulfilling prophecy. In its contemporary form, labeling theory proposes reforms that focus on reducing stigma, implementing restorative justice practices, and providing support for reintegration into society. In that perspective, an integrated approach such as restorative justice can be seen as trying to transform both the individual and society. Restorative justice focuses on repairing the harm caused by crime through reconciliation between victims and offenders, community involvement, and restorative practices that promote healing and reintegration.

Finally, opportunity-based theories also known as the situational approach—which include, for instance, the routine activities approach (Cohen & Felson, 1979), the contemporary version of rational choice theory (Cornish & Clarke, 1986; Clarke & Felson, 1993), crime pattern theory (Brantingham & Brantingham, 1984), environmental criminology (Brantingham & Brantingham, 1991; Bottoms & Wiles, 1997), and broken windows theory (Wilson & Kelling, 1982; Kelling & Coles, 1996)—do not seek to directly change individuals or social structures but to improve society by reducing crime and the fear of crime. By focusing on the immediate environmental factors that create opportunities for crime, situational crime prevention offers a pragmatic approach to enhancing public safety and quality of life. The benefits of situational crime prevention are numerous. By redesigning urban spaces, increasing surveillance, and hardening potential targets, this approach can significantly reduce the incidence of crime in specific locations. This, in turn, can help to reduce the fear of crime among residents and visitors, allowing them to more fully enjoy and participate in public life. In addition, by deterring future offenders, it can improve the life of these persons that can avoid suffering the legal consequences of committing a crime. Moreover, by reducing the overall level of crime in a society, situational crime prevention can help to alleviate the burden on the criminal justice system, freeing up resources for other important social needs.

In sum, criminological theories aim to bring about change in individuals, society, the criminal justice system, or the environment by addressing the root causes of criminal behavior through a combination of punishment, rehabilitation, social support, environmental design, and systemic reforms. These theories are rooted in the belief that humankind can change and move toward gradual betterment, which aligns with a progressive ethos. That is why one can argue that the ethos of criminology is progressive.

The Debate Between Reform-Oriented and Problem-Solving Criminologists

Despite the progressive ethos that underlies much of criminology, not all criminological theories and approaches are equally embraced within the field. In particular, those who advocate for problem-solving criminology often find themselves criticized by reform-oriented criminologists, who view them as conservative, administrative, or actuarial in their approach. These critiques argue that opportunity-based theories fail to address the root causes of crime—among which they tend to prioritize poverty, inequality, and social marginalization—and do not seek to fundamentally change either the individual offender or the broader society. As problem-solving criminology is often associated with a pragmatic, policy-oriented approach to crime control and prevention, critiques consider that it has a narrow focus, lacks theoretical depth, neglects social justice issues, has a technocratic approach, has an overreliance on quantitative methods, has ethical concerns, fails to address power structures, and has short-term focus. Problem-solving criminologists respond to criticisms by emphasizing the practical, evidence-based nature of their work, the balance between control and prevention, the integration of social justice considerations, the use of comprehensive methodologies, the inclusion of ethical safeguards, and the potential for both short-term and long-term positive impacts on crime and public safety. They argue that their approaches are based on rigorous empirical research and have often been shown to effectively reduce crime in targeted areas. They also emphasize that situational crime prevention strategies can be implemented alongside other efforts to address social and economic inequalities and that reducing crime can help to improve the quality of life for disadvantaged communities.

A good example of this debate refers to the situation in the United Kingdom, where criminologists working for the Home Office were being accused of doing "administrative criminology." The best summary and answer to these critiques is that of Patricia Mayhew (2016) based on her common speech with Ronald Clarke, when they receive the Stockholm Prize of Criminology, which is the equivalent of a Nobel Prize in criminology. According to Mayhew (2016), a former UK Home Office researcher, "administrative criminology" has been criticized in two main ways: first, as being too narrowly focused on situational crime prevention (SCP) in the 1980s and more recently as conducting atheoretical, narrowly focused evaluations to support the current political agenda. Mayhew argues that SCP, developed by researchers in the Home Office in the 1970s–1980s, was intellectually grounded and influential, despite facing initial resistance. Other influential Home Office research included policing studies and the British Crime Survey. She contends that the alleged shortcomings of more recent administrative criminology reflect increasing government control over research rather than inherent flaws. Earlier administrative criminology was largely researcher-driven, vibrant and often controversial. Administrative criminology makes important contributions by collecting essential data through surveys on victimization and offending and compiling national crime statistics. This empirical data is used by all types of criminologists. Administrative criminologists emphasize effective communication of research findings to policy-makers and practitioners. As a result, their work tends to be more influential on policy than academic criminology. While the explanatory focus may have narrowed, Mayhew argues administrative criminology still deserves a positive appraisal for its past achievements and ongoing contributions to the field. A degree of criminological pluralism should be encouraged (Mayhew, 2016).

In that context, one can argue that situational crime prevention, while differing in specific methods and focus from other criminological approaches, shares a fundamental commitment to improving society by reducing crime. Rather than being viewed as opposed to other progressive criminological theories, situational crime prevention should be seen as complementary. By addressing the immediate environmental factors that contribute to crime, situational crime prevention helps create the conditions necessary for other progressive reforms, such as rehabilitation, restorative justice, and social justice, to take root and flourish.

In conclusion, while situational crime prevention may be criticized by some within the field of criminology as being conservative or administrative in its approach, it is in fact deeply progressive in its orientation. By seeking to reduce crime and the fear of crime through practical, evidence-based interventions, situational crime prevention offers a valuable tool for improving society and enhancing public safety. Rather than being dismissed or marginalized, situational crime prevention should be embraced as an important component of a comprehensive, progressive approach to addressing the problem of crime in modern society.

Challenges and Limitations of the Progressive Ethos in Criminology: The Offline Crime Drop in the United States as a Case Study

The debate about the causes of the drop of offline offenses in the United States in the 1990s can serve as a good example of the arguments developed previously. In 1997, William J. Bratton, who had been the New York City Police Commissioner from 1994 to 1996, published an influential essay entitled "Crime is Down in New York City: Blame the police" included in a book edited by Norman Dennis (1997, 1998). In January 1998, in his speech on the State of the Union, President Clinton adopted the same point of view and stated that the crime drop that was beginning to take place in the United States was due to the policies of his government (for details, see the next chapter of this book). Immediately after, criminologists started proposing alternatives explanations.

In that context, Felson (2000) stated: "In the United States, in response to the decrease in crime rates, the police and politicians immediately claimed all the credit for themselves. These same claims have been contested by academic criminologists, who have denied them any credit. The truth probably lies somewhere in between" (translated from Italian by us). The trouble of course is how to find that middle point.

In particular, the first explanations of the crime drop in the United States were summarized in two key compilations: issue 88/4 of the *Journal of Criminal Law and Criminology* published in 1998 and a 2000 book in Italian edited by Marzio Barbagli (2000). Barbagli's book is particularly remarkable for its extensive introduction, in which the author successfully combines various factors to propose a comprehensive explanation for the crime drop. The book, and specifically Barbagli's introduction, was reviewed by a sociologist (Massari, 2000) in an article that exemplifies the type of reaction from "academic criminologists" in the terminology of Felson (2000) or "reform-oriented" criminologists or sociologists according to the terminology proposed in this chapter. Massari (2000) states:

> Explanations of the crime decline centered on the role of specific penal policies and policing strategies adopted in some American cities appear partial. The case of New York—widely cited by various scholars in this volume as the only success example in crime trends—represents a perhaps obvious but certainly paradigmatic observatory. The de facto criminalization of a range of social and subcultural behaviors induced by the zero-tolerance policy, along with the adoption of control strategies heavily inspired by racial profiling—evident in practices like stopping and searching cars based on the race of the driver or passengers—has contributed significantly to spreading both a strong fear of the police and increasing ethnic and racial tensions. The issue of discriminatory attitudes adopted by police in numerous states has gained increasing importance in recent years, given the proposal of a law in Congress that would require police officers to compile statistics containing information on stopped vehicles, particularly the race or ethnicity of the driver and occupants. Despite Barbagli informing us that 'in the United States, the percentage of people who give a positive judgment on the police's work is higher than in any other Western country' (p. 41), it is impossible to ignore the constant increase in complaints of police brutality, unwarranted arrests, and civil rights violations. In most cases, as non-governmental organizations for human rights protection inform us, brutality incidents target individuals belonging to an ethnic or racial minority (Human Rights Watch World Report, 2002). However, in other major U.S. cities, the same successes were achieved through policies focused on the contextual responsibility of both citizens and authorities, collaboration with neighborhoods, parishes, and black churches, the presence of support and volunteer groups, probation control strategies, and mediation mechanisms aimed at avoiding judicial paths. It is precisely on these anti-New York models, such as Boston, Washington, and San Diego, that we would have liked to read more in the volume's essays. (Massari, 2000: 7–8, translated from Italian by us)

Massari's review focuses less on the content of Barbagli's book and more on promoting the view that the decrease in crime rates should be attributed primarily to socioeconomic factors rather than policing strategies. This is particularly evident in her critique of the policing strategies inspired by the broken windows theory, which she labels as "zero-tolerance" policies. Massari (2000) argues that attributing the crime decline to these aggressive policing strategies oversimplifies and misrepresents the broader socioeconomic dynamics involved. She emphasizes the negative impacts of zero-tolerance policies, such as the potential to exacerbate racial and socioeconomic disparities and the erosion of civil liberties. While acknowledging that some police departments may have implemented innovative practices on a small scale, Massari contends that these efforts are often too limited to account for the widespread crime reduction. In contrast, Barbagli's introduction is not solely based on the essays in the book he edited but also on those in the volume by

Blumstein and Wallman (2000) and an extensive review of relevant literature (Barbagli, 2000). This scenario illustrates an author striving to provide a holistic explanation of crime trends while a reviewer pushes to impose an alternative perspective that dismisses a significant portion of the author's potential explanation and prescribes how the latter should have approached the issue.

This example of 2000 reminds us also of the perennity of the debate about the role of the police in society. Reform-oriented criminologists often call for greater police accountability and oversight, and some even advocate for defunding or abolishing the police altogether. However, problem-solving criminologists can argue that the police play a crucial role in maintaining public safety and that efforts to diminish their authority could have unintended consequences, again the unending debate between reform-oriented and problem-solving criminologists.

Conclusion

Throughout this chapter, the historical roots of the progressive ethos in criminology have been explored, tracing its origins to the philosophical discourse on progress and scientific advancement that emerged during the Enlightenment. It has been shown how these ideas influenced the development of criminological theories and approaches, from the early classical school's focus on rational deterrence and proportional punishment to the contemporary debates between reform-oriented and problem-solving criminologists.

In the context of that debate, the challenges and limitations of the progressive ethos in criminology have also been examined. While reform-oriented approaches emphasize the need for broad societal changes to address the underlying causes of crime, problem-solving approaches, such as situational crime prevention, focus on more targeted, evidence-based strategies to reduce specific crime types and improve public safety. The debate surrounding the crime drop in the United States served as a prime example of the tensions between these two perspectives and how adopting one perspective can lead to a skewed view of a phenomenon.

In this perspective, it seems crucial for contemporary researchers and practitioners to recognize the strengths and limitations of both reform-oriented and problem-solving approaches. By fostering constructive dialogue and embracing a more inclusive and integrative perspective, criminologists can work toward a comprehensive understanding of crime and its prevention. As new challenges arise, such as those presented by living in a hybrid society, criminologists from both perspectives could strive to find common ground, adapting their theories and methods to address these complex issues. Ultimately, the progressive ethos in criminology underscores the field's commitment to understanding and improving the human condition through the application of reason and empirical research. This work has the potential to inform public policy, shape criminal justice practices, and influence societal attitudes toward crime and justice.

References

Barbagli, M. (Ed.). (2000). *Perché è diminuita la criminalità negli Stati Uniti?* Il Mulino.

Beccaria, C. (2009/1764). *On Crimes and Punishments* (5th ed., Translation, annotations, and introduction by G. R. Newman and P. Marongiu). Transaction Publishers, 2009 (Original work published 1764).

Blumstein, A., & Wallman, J. (Eds.). (2000). *The crime drop in America*. Cambridge University Press.

Bottoms, A. E., & Wiles, P. (1997). Environmental criminology. In M. Maguire, R. Morgan, & R. Reiner (Eds.), *The Oxford handbook of criminology* (pp. 305–359). Oxford University Press.

Brantingham, P. J., & Brantingham, P. L. (1984). *Patterns in crime*. Macmillan.

Brantingham, P. L., & Brantingham, P. J. (1991). *Environmental criminology*. Waveland Press.

Bristow, W. (2024). Enlightenment. In E. N. Zalta & U. Nodelman (Eds.), *The Stanford Encyclopedia of Philosophy (Spring 2024 Edition)*. Stanford University. https://plato.stanford.edu/archives/spr2024/entries/enlightenment/

Britannica, T. Editors of Encyclopaedia. (2024, January 27). *Reign of Terror*. Encyclopedia Britannica. https://www.britannica.com/event/Reign-of-Terror

Clarke, R. V. G., & Felson, M. (1993). *Routine activity and rational choice*. Transaction Publishers.

Cohen, L. E., & Felson, M. (1979). Social change and crime rate trends: A routine activity approach. *American Sociological Review, 44*(4), 588–608. https://doi.org/10.2307/2094589

Comte, A. (1830). *Cours de philosophie positive. Tome premier contenant les préliminaires généraux et la philosophie mathématique*. Rouen frères; au dépôt de la Librairie médicale française.

Cornish, D. B., & Clarke, R. V. (1986). *The reasoning criminal: Rational choice perspectives on offending*. Springer.

Cusson, M. (2024). Personal communication (11 June 2024).

Dennis, N. (Ed.). (1997). *Zero tolerance: Policing a free society*. IEA Health and Welfare Unit.

Dennis, N. (Ed.). (1998). *Zero tolerance: Policing a free society. Enlarged and revised* (2nd ed.). IEA Health and Welfare Unit.

Felson, M. (2000). Trend e cicli del tasso di criminalità: I cambiamenti nella società moderna. In M. Barbagli (Ed.), *Perché è diminuita la criminalità negli Stati Uniti?* (pp. 89–107). Il Mulino.

Hamilton, A. (2020). "Conservatism", *The Stanford Encyclopedia of Philosophy* (Spring 2020 Edition), Edward N. Zalta (ed.). https://plato.stanford.edu/archives/spr2020/entries/conservatism/

Harper's Magazine. (2020, July 7). A letter on justice and open debate. *Harper's Magazine*. https://harpers.org/a-letter-on-justice-and-open-debate/

Human Rights Watch Staff. (2002). *World Report 2002: Events of 2001, November 2000-November 2001*. Human Rights Watch. https://www.hrw.org/legacy/wr2k1/

Kelling, G. L., & Coles, C. M. (1996). *Fixing broken windows: Restoring order and reducing crime in our communities*. Free Press.

Kuhn, T. S. (1970). *The structure of scientific revolutions* (2nd ed., enlarged). The University of Chicago Press. (First edition 1962).

Laudan, L. (1977). *Progress and its problems: Towards a theory of scientific growth*. Routledge & Kegan Paul.

Massari, M. (2000). Punizione e pregiudizio: l'andamento della criminalità negli Stati Uniti. *Quaderni di Sociologia, 23*, 149–157. http://journals.openedition.org/qds/1370. https://doi.org/10.4000/qds.1370

Mayhew, P. (2016). In defence of administrative criminology. *Crime Science, 5*, 1–10.

Newman, G. R. (1997). Criminology and policing. In P. Beirne & D. Nelken (Eds.), *Issues in Comparative Criminology* (pp. 181–189). Ashgate/Dartmouth. (Original work published 1988).

Niiniluoto, I. (2024). Scientific progress. In E. N. Zalta & U. Nodelman (Eds.), *The Stanford Encyclopedia of Philosophy (Spring 2024 Edition)*. Stanford University. https://plato.stanford.edu/archives/spr2024/entries/scientific-progress/

Paradox Politics. (2021, February 4; updated: 2023, August 7). Noam Chomsky cancel culture Harper's letter. *Paradox Politics*. https://paradoxpolitics.com/2021/02/noam-chomsky-cancel-culture-harpers-letter/

Pinker, S. (2018). *Enlightenment now: The case for reason, science, humanism, and progress*. Viking.

Popper, K. R. (1957). *The poverty of historicism*. Routledge and Kegan Paul. (Original work published 1944–1945).

Popper, K. R. (1959). *The logic of scientific discovery*. Basic Books. (Original work published in German in 1934).

Quetelet, A. (1835). *Sur l'homme et le développement de ses facultés ou Essai de physique sociale*. Bachelier.

Quinney, R. (1974). *Critique of legal order: Crime control in capitalist society*. Little, Brown and Company.

Quinney, R. (1979). *Class, state, and crime: On the theory and practice of criminal justice*. Longman.

Scott, J., & Marshall, G. (2015). *A dictionary of sociology* (4th ed.). Oxford University Press. https://www.oxfordreference.com/display/10.1093/acref/9780199683581.001.0001/acref-9780199683581

Spitzer, S. (1975). Toward a Marxian theory of deviance. *Social Problems, 22*(5), 638–651.

Tam, A., & Meek Lange, M. (2024). Progress. In E. N. Zalta & U. Nodelman (Eds.), *The Stanford Encyclopedia of Philosophy (Spring 2024 Edition)*. Stanford University. https://plato.stanford.edu/archives/spr2024/entries/progress/

Taylor, I., Walton, P., & Young, J. (1973). *The new criminology: For a social theory of deviance*. Routledge & Kegan Paul.

Voltaire. (1759). *Candide, ou l'optimisme*. Gabriel Cramer.

Wilson, J. Q., & Kelling, G. L. (1982). Broken Windows: The Police and Neighborhood Safety. *Atlantic Monthly, 249*(3), 29–38.

Open Access This chapter is licensed under the terms of the Creative Commons Attribution 4.0 International License (http://creativecommons.org/licenses/by/4.0/), which permits use, sharing, adaptation, distribution and reproduction in any medium or format, as long as you give appropriate credit to the original author(s) and the source, provide a link to the Creative Commons license and indicate if changes were made.

The images or other third party material in this chapter are included in the chapter's Creative Commons license, unless indicated otherwise in a credit line to the material. If material is not included in the chapter's Creative Commons license and your intended use is not permitted by statutory regulation or exceeds the permitted use, you will need to obtain permission directly from the copyright holder.

Chapter 2
A Narrative Review of the Debate on the So-Called International Crime Drop

Marcelo F. Aebi

The Rise of a Concept: The International Crime Drop

The concept of an "international crime drop" emerged from observations of declining crime rates in Western industrialized nations during the 1990s and 2000s. This phenomenon first gained attention in the United States, where a significant decrease in crime rates was observed starting in the early 1990s. To fully understand the development of this concept, it is crucial to examine the context in which it arose and the data that initially supported it.

The American Context

In 1991, the United States reached a peak in its homicide rate, with 9.8 murders per 100,000 inhabitants. This marked the culmination of a period of high crime rates that had persisted throughout the 1980s, causing significant public concern and political debate. However, the years that followed saw a dramatic shift in this trend.

By 1993, the homicide rate had decreased to 9.5 per 100,000, a modest reduction that could have been seen as a random fluctuation in the short term. However, the downward trend continued and accelerated. By 1995, the rate had fallen to 8.2, and by 1996, it was down to 7.4, clearly indicating a significant downward trend.

This decline was not limited to homicide. Other types of crime, particularly property crimes, also showed substantial decreases. According to the FBI's Uniform

---

M. F. Aebi (✉)
School of Criminal Sciences, Faculty of Law, Criminal Sciences and Public Administration, University of Lausanne, Lausanne, Switzerland
e-mail: marcelo.aebi@unil.ch

Crime Reports, the rate of property crime fell by 30.8% between 1991 and 2000, while the violent crime rate decreased by 33.2% over the same period.

These dramatic reductions in crime rates caught the attention of criminologists, policymakers, and the media. The phenomenon came to be known as the "crime drop," and it sparked intense debate and research as experts sought to understand its causes and implications.

Expansion to Other Countries

As researchers began to analyze this trend, they discovered similar patterns in other English-speaking countries, particularly the United Kingdom and Australia. In the United Kingdom, for example, the British Crime Survey showed that crime peaked in 1995 and then fell by 33% between 1995 and 2004/2005.

This apparent similarity in trends across different countries led to the formulation of the "international crime drop" concept. The idea was that the crime decline observed in the United States was not an isolated phenomenon but part of a broader international trend affecting many developed countries.

Complexities and Variations

However, as the debate evolved and more data from a wider range of countries became available, it became clear that the picture was more complex than initially thought, especially when considering countries in continental Europe.

While some types of offenses, particularly homicide and offline property crimes, indeed diminished in many Western industrialized nations, trends in other violent crimes were more diverse. For instance, many continental Western European countries experienced increases in certain violent crimes during the same period when the United States was seeing declines.

Moreover, the rise of online offenses, an inevitable consequence of the digital age, was largely overlooked in the initial formulations of the crime drop concept. This omission would later become a point of contention in the academic debate, as researchers began to question whether the apparent drop in traditional offline crimes might be partially offset by increases in cybercrime.

Challenges to the Concept

As more data became available and researchers conducted more sophisticated analyses, several challenges to the concept of an "international crime drop" emerged. These included the following: (a) Variation across crime types: While property crimes and homicide showed consistent declines in many countries, other types of violent crime, such as assault and robbery, showed more varied trends. (b) Regional differences: The patterns observed in the United States and other English-speaking countries were not always replicated in continental Europe or other parts of the world. (c) Data quality and comparability: Differences in legal definitions, reporting practices, and data collection methods across countries made direct comparisons challenging. (d) The rise of cybercrime: The growth of internet-related offenses raised questions about whether crime was truly declining or merely shifting to new forms. (e) Temporal variations: The timing and magnitude of crime declines varied across countries, suggesting that if there was an international trend, it was not uniform.

These challenges led to a more nuanced understanding of crime trends and a recognition that the concept of an "international crime drop" might be an oversimplification of a complex phenomenon.

The aim of this chapter is to establish a timeline of the debates about the international dimension of the so-called crime drop and to present four narratives that represent four different interpretations of the trends observed.

A Timeline of the Debate on the International Crime Drop

To better understand the evolution of this debate, it is helpful to consider a timeline of key events and publications. This timeline not only charts the development of the "international crime drop" concept but also highlights the growing complexity of the academic discourse surrounding it.

1997–1998: The Initial Recognition

The concept of a significant crime decline gained initial traction with the publication of "Zero Tolerance: Policing a Free Society" (Dennis, 1997, 1998). This collection includes William J. Bratton's influential essay on crime reduction in New York City, which attributes the city's dramatic crime decline to changes in policing strategies inspired by the broken window approach (Wilson & Kelling, 1982). Bratton's essay, while focused on New York, helps set the stage for broader discussions about crime trends.

1998: Political Recognition

In January 1998, US President Bill Clinton's 1998 delivers his State of the Union speech stating:

> A society rooted in responsibility must provide safe streets, safe schools, and safe neighborhoods. We pursued a strategy of more police, tougher punishment, smarter prevention, with crimefighting partnerships with local law enforcement and citizen groups, where the rubber hits the road. I can report to you tonight that it's working. Violent crime is down; robbery is down; assault is down; burglary is down—for 5 years in a row, all across America. We need to finish the job of putting 100,000 more police on our streets (source: https://www.presidency.ucsb.edu/documents/address-before-joint-session-the-congress-the-state-the-union-8).

These events accelerate the debate on the crime drop in the United States. A conference is organized, and the papers presented in it are compiled in issue 88/4 of the *Journal of Criminal Law and Criminology* published in 1998 (Travis, 1998).

1999: International Perspectives Emerge

The Cattaneo Institute in Bologna, Italy, hosts a seminar of international experts, bringing together scholars from the United States and Europe to discuss crime trends. This meeting leads to the publication of *Perché è diminuita la criminalità negli Stati Uniti?* (Why Has Crime Decreased in the United States?) in 2000, edited by Marzio Barbagli. This collection represents the first attempts to examine the US crime drop from an international perspective and includes a first Italian version of Killias and Aebi (2000a) paper suggestively subtitled "How Europe Illustrates the Limits of the American Experience" (Killias & Aebi, 2000b).

2000: Expanding the Discourse

Several significant publications appear this year, broadening the debate:

- A special issue of the *European Journal on Criminal Policy and Research* focuses on "Crime Trends in Europe," providing a more comprehensive look at crime patterns across the continent (Killias & Jehle, 2000).
- The first edition of *The Crime Drop in America* by Alfred Blumstein and Joel Wallman is published, offering a detailed examination of the US crime decline and potential explanations (Blumstein & Wallman, 2000).
- Marzio Barbagli publishes *Perché è diminuita la criminalità negli Stati Uniti?* (Why Has Crime Decreased in the United States?) (Barbagli, 2000).

These publications help establish the crime drop as a major topic of criminological research and begin to explore its potential international dimensions.

2004: Cross-National Studies and Eastern European Perspectives

This year sees the publication of two important volumes:

- *Cross-National Studies in Crime and Justice* edited by David P. Farrington, Patrick A. Langan, and Michael Tonry, which provides comparative analyses of crime trends across several countries (Farrington et al., 2004).
- A special issue of the *European Journal on Criminal Policy and Research* on "Crime trends in Western and Eastern European countries," edited by Marcelo F. Aebi. This issue is particularly significant as it includes perspectives from Eastern Europe, broadening the geographical scope of the debate (Aebi, 2004).

2005: Comprehensive Analysis of Western Countries

The publication of *Crime and Justice, Volume 33: Crime and Punishment in Western Countries, 1980–1999* edited by Michael Tonry and David P. Farrington represents a major milestone. This volume provides a detailed examination of crime trends across several Western countries over two decades, offering one of the most comprehensive comparative analyses to date (Tonry & Farrington, 2005a).

2007: Victimization Perspective

Jan van Dijk, John van Kesteren, and Paul Smit publish *Criminal Victimisation in International Perspective*, based on the International Crime Victims Survey. This book provides valuable insights into crime trends from the perspective of victims across multiple countries, offering a different angle on the crime drop phenomenon (van Dijk et al., 2007).

2010: Challenging the Universality

Marcelo F. Aebi and Antonia Linde publish "Is There a Crime Drop in Western Europe?" in the *European Journal on Criminal Policy and Research*. This paper challenges the universality of the crime drop concept, highlighting divergent trends across different types of offenses and countries in Western Europe. It marks a significant moment in the debate, introducing more skepticism about the idea of a uniform international crime drop (Aebi & Linde, 2010).

2012: New Directions in Research

The publication of *The International Crime Drop: New Directions in Research* edited by Jan van Dijk, Andromachi Tseloni, and Graham Farrell represents a major consolidation of various perspectives on the topic. This book brings together researchers from different countries and theoretical backgrounds, providing a comprehensive overview of the state of research on the international crime drop (van Dijk et al., 2012).

2014: Comprehensive Review and Theoretical Developments

Crime and Justice, Volume 43: Why Crime Rates Fall, and Why They Don't edited by Michael Tonry is published. This volume provides a comprehensive overview of the debate, including various theoretical explanations for crime declines and examinations of trends in different countries. It also includes critical perspectives that question some of the assumptions underlying the international crime drop concept (Tonry, 2014a).

2018: Bringing Crime Trends Back into Criminology

Several significant publications appear this year:

- A special issue of the *European Journal on Criminal Policy and Research* on "Crime and Criminal Justice in Europe," edited by Marcelo F. Aebi and Jörg-Martin Jehle, provides updated analyses of crime trends across Europe (Aebi & Jehle, 2018).
- Eric P. Baumer, María B. Vélez, and Richard Rosenfeld publish "Bringing Crime Trends Back into Criminology: A Critical Assessment of the Literature and a Blueprint for Future Inquiry" in the *Annual Review of Criminology*. This paper provides a critical review of research on crime trends in the United States, ignoring bluntly all research conducted elsewhere and at an international level. A surprising level of parochialism considering that the first and third author had participated in several of the events mentioned in this timeline and dedicated to study the similarities and differences in the crime trends observed in the United States and in Europe (Baumer et al., 2018).

The timeline illustrates the evolution of the debate from an initial focus on the American experience to a broader international perspective. In the subsequent sections, the four major narratives on crime trends during the 1990s and 2000s will be presented. These narratives are categorized as (a) all-American narratives, (b) the Lausanne school narrative, (c) the *Crime and Justice* narrative, and (d) the security hypothesis narrative. The first narrative explores the consensus in the United States regarding crime trends while highlighting divergent interpretations. The other three narratives concentrate on international crime trends, discussing divergences in the interpretation of nonlethal violent offenses, the impact of cybercrime, and potential explanations for the decline in offline property offenses beyond the commonly accepted opportunity-based theories.

The All-American Narratives

The study of crime trends in the United States has been a cornerstone of criminological research, often setting the tone for global discussions on the topic. This "All-American" perspective has been both influential and, at times, limiting in our understanding of international crime patterns.

As Baumer et al. (2018) comprehensively reviewed, the United States has experienced not one but multiple "Great American Crime Declines" (Zimring, 2007). These declines have varied significantly across offense types, data sources, and demographic factors, painting a complex picture that challenges simplistic narratives. The story begins in the early 1980s when property crimes started their downward trajectory. Interestingly, the National Crime Victimization Survey (NCVS) data shows that rape and aggravated assault also began to decline around this time, a trend not immediately reflected in official police statistics. This discrepancy highlights the importance of using multiple data sources in crime trend analysis, a methodological approach that has been a hallmark of American research.

Homicide, often considered the most reliable indicator of violent crime, presents a particularly nuanced picture. While general homicide rates began to fall in the early 1990s—a trend that captured much public and scholarly attention—a closer look reveals important variations. Homicide rates for adults aged 30 and over, as well as for females, had already begun to decrease as early as 1980. In contrast, homicide rates for adolescents and young adults followed a different pattern, rising from the mid-1980s, peaking in the early 1990s, and then declining sharply (Baumer et al., 2018).

These varied trends underscore a key lesson from the American experience: the danger of overgeneralization. What might appear as a uniform "crime drop" is, in reality, a complex interplay of different trends for different crimes and different population subgroups.

Despite the wealth of data and research, Baumer et al. (2018) argue that criminologists have struggled to develop a robust scientific understanding of these trends. They identify two main reasons for this shortcoming. First, many explanations focus on single factors rather than considering multiple, interacting causes. Second, the study of crime trends has often been disconnected from broader criminological theory, limiting our understanding of the underlying mechanisms.

To address these limitations, Baumer et al. (2018) propose a conceptual framework that organizes explanations around three key mechanisms: changes in social controls, shifts in criminal propensities and motivations, and alterations in exposure to criminogenic settings. This framework attempts to integrate crime trends research with mainstream criminological theory, a step toward a more comprehensive understanding.

Accordingly, Baumer et al. (2018) place the available explanations of the offline crime drop in the United States withing these three mechanisms. First, explanations emphasizing increased social control include a growth in immigration, increased community cohesion and stronger social institutions, increased government trust, growth in police forces and enhanced policing strategies, enhanced security measures, and increase in imprisonment. Second, explanations focusing on reductions in criminal propensity and motivation include the legalization of abortion, reduction in lead exposure, aging population, growth in economic opportunities and performance, stabilization of illicit drug markets, and reduction in substance abuse. Third, explanations highlighting reduced exposure to criminogenic settings and situations include increased time spent at home and away from public spaces and the stabilization of illicit and secondary markets (Baumer et al., 2018).

In sum, the American narrative offers a wide range of explanations for the observed crime drops. In fact, it is crucial to note that despite decades of research, there remains no consensus on the exact causes of the crime drop in the United States. This lack of consensus in a country where the existence of a significant offline crime drop is undisputed underscores the challenges in explaining crime trends, let alone generalizing these explanations to other national contexts.

Consequently, the dominance of these American narratives in global criminological discourse raises important questions. Why have these perspectives been so influential internationally, despite their focus on US-specific factors? How applicable are these explanations to other national contexts with different social, political, and economic realities?

The Lausanne School Narrative

Since the late 1980s, criminologists affiliated with the School of Criminal Justice at the University of Lausanne have been conducting extensive research in comparative criminology, hence contributing to the debate on international crime trends. Their work has been instrumental in developing large datasets for comparative research, including the European Sourcebook of Crime and Criminal Justice Statistics, with seven editions as of 2024,[1] and the Council of Europe Annual Penal Statistics, better known as the SPACE statistics.[2] These datasets provide an empirical foundation for analyzing crime trends across Europe and beyond.

---

[1] See CoE (1999), Killias et al. (2003), and Aebi et al. (2006, 2010, 2014, 2021, 2024).
[2] See, for example, Aebi et al. (2019a, b, c).

The Lausanne School's approach is characterized by a focus on empirical data, a critical examination of existing theories, and an emphasis on understanding regional contexts. Their work has consistently challenged overly simplistic narratives about crime trends, highlighting the complex and often divergent patterns observed across different crime types and geographical regions. Their explanations of the trends observed draw mainly on opportunity-based theories, proposing multifactor models that combine the routine activities approach (Cohen & Felson, 1979) with lifestyle theory (Hindelang et al., 1978) and take into account the digital revolution that started in the last quarter of the twentieth century and led to our contemporary hybrid society. The key publications and contributions from this school are presented in the following sections.

Crime Trends in Europe from 1990 to 1996: How Europe Illustrates the Limits of the American Experience (Killias & Aebi, 2000a)

Killias and Aebi (2000a) analyzed crime trends in 36 European countries between 1990 and 1996, comparing them to the declining trends in the United States during the same period. In Europe, the study found that while property offenses showed a pattern of increase followed by decrease, violent offenses generally increased, and drug offenses rose substantially.

Killias and Aebi (2000a) challenged the applicability of US-centric explanations to European contexts. They argued that many factors proposed to explain the US crime drop, such as changes in policing strategies or demographic shifts, did not align well with European data.[3] Instead, and in line with Felson (1998, 1999), they suggested that situational explanations like the routine activities approach were more useful for understanding the observed trends.

The authors highlighted the impact of significant political changes, particularly the fall of communist regimes and the opening of borders between Eastern and Western Europe in 1989. These events likely created new criminal opportunities influencing trends in theft, drug trafficking, and violence. This work served as an early indication that the crime drop was not a universal phenomenon and set the stage for more nuanced analyses of international crime trends.

---

[3] For a presentation of these explanations, see Barbagli (2000) and issue 88/4 of the *Journal of Criminal Law and Criminology* (Travis, 1998).

Crime Trends in Western Europe from 1990 to 2000 (Aebi, 2004b)

Aebi (2004b) expanded on the previous work, analyzing crime trends for nine offenses in 16 Western European countries from 1990 to 2000. This study confirmed and extended the earlier findings, showing that property offenses peaked around 1992 before decreasing, while nonlethal violent offenses and drug offenses increased steadily throughout the decade.

The author insisted on the relevance of opportunity-based theories to explain these trends, emphasizing how changes in daily routines and opportunities for crime have been influenced by the political and economic changes after 1989. He argued that the abolition of borders between East and West Europe facilitated the development of illegal routes for goods, drugs, and even persons, contributing to the emergence of organized crime networks. The decrease in property crimes after the early 1990s peak is partly attributed by Aebi (2004) to the saturation of black markets in Eastern Europe combined with enhanced security measures in Western European households. The rise in violence is partially attributed to conflicts over illegal markets and the consolidation of marginalized ethnic neighborhoods. The steady rise of drug offenses mirrors increases in drug use indicated by other data sources in Western Europe. This trend likely reflects greater drug availability in European markets.

Aebi (2004b) also critically examined alternative explanations, rejecting those based on social bonding theory, anomie, and subcultural theories as insufficient to explain the observed patterns. Regarding the latter, he applied a historical-comparative approach to show that the Italian American Mafia in the United States was influenced more by the opportunity structure (e.g., the prohibition) than by subcultural factors because the same Italian migrants moved to Argentina without developing such a criminal network. Seven years later, Varese (2011) would test and corroborate a similar hypothesis.

The same year, Aebi (2004a) published an updated version of the plenary conference he had pronounced in 2003 at the Third Conference of the European Society of Criminology in Helsinki, expanding his analyses to cover Eastern Europe. In this region, from 1990 to 2000, drug offenses exploded; violent crimes peaked mid-decade but were decreasing by 2000, except for robbery which continued rising; and property crimes generally increased throughout the decade. In line with his previous works, the author attributed these trends largely to political and economic changes following the fall of communism in 1989, which created new criminal opportunities across Europe.

Is There a Crime Drop in Western Europe? (Aebi & Linde, 2010)

Aebi and Linde (2010) analyzed crime trends in 14 West European countries from 1990 to 2007, utilizing both police statistics and victimization surveys. The study found that while property crimes and homicide generally decreased, violent crimes showed divergent trends, with assault increasing substantially and robbery showing fluctuations. Drug offenses increased steadily throughout the period.

Aebi and Linde (2010) proposed a multifactor explanation for these trends, introducing several elements: (a) changes in criminal opportunities following the fall of the Soviet Union; (b) improved security measures and growth of private security; (c) changes in youth lifestyles due to internet use; (d) increases in binge drinking among youth; (e) the development of street gangs, mainly composed of second-generation migrants in some areas; and (f) improvements in medical technology and health services that played a crucial role in reducing the lethality of aggressions, contributing to the decrease in homicide rates despite the increase in assaults.

To the best of our knowledge, this paper was the first to introduce the impact of changes in youth lifestyles due to internet use in the context of international crime trends. The authors made a crucial distinction between youths with full internet access and those without, predating the widespread adoption of smartphones, which would arrive only in 2007.

Linde and Aebi (2015) presented their multifactor model with more detail in a chapter included in a book honoring Marcus Felson, arguing that routine activity theory can be applied at a macrosocial level to explain divergent trends in different types of crimes. The key elements of their multifactorial model include (1) increased youth internet access, which reduced time spent in public spaces and opportunities for certain offline crimes; (2) growth in the proportion of young foreign residents, potentially leading to increased youth gangs and violence in some areas; (3) changes in alcohol consumption patterns among youth, including the impact of binge drinking; and (4) for property crime specifically, an initial increase in the early 1990s in some Eastern European countries due to new criminal opportunities, followed by a subsequent decrease from the mid-1990s onward, attributed to (a) improved security measures, (b) growth of private security services, and (c) improved socioeconomic conditions in Central and Eastern Europe. Linde and Aebi (2015) contend that this model, grounded in routine activity theory, can account for the seemingly contradictory trends observed in different crime types across Western Europe during this period. They argue that changes in everyday activities and opportunity structures, rather than changes in criminal motivations, best explain the observed crime patterns.

Fifteen years later, the two major changes to that model are the impact of the arrival of smartphones, which democratized the access to the internet, and the decrease in alcohol consumption even if heavy drinking episodes are still present in many European countries.[4] At the same time, violence among gangs of second- and third-generation ethnic minorities led to huge increases in homicides in Sweden,[5] and other Nordic countries are not far behind.[6] Indeed, street gang violence is a growing concern in EU countries.[7]

Conviction Statistics as an Indicator of Crime Trends (Aebi & Linde, 2012a)

Aebi and Linde (2012a) analyzed conviction statistics for six offenses in up to 26 European countries from 1990 to 2006. The findings corroborated earlier results using police statistics, showing decreases in property offenses and homicides, increases in nonlethal violent offenses, and dramatic increases in drug offenses.

The authors concluded that their results supported their previous multifactor explanation based on opportunity theories (Aebi & Linde, 2010). Aebi and Linde (2012a) considered that there was no *general* crime drop in continental Europe. Rather, trends vary by offense type and region. The authors argue their findings highlight the need for contextualized analyses of crime patterns that consider the unique historical and social factors in different parts of Europe.

Crime Trends in Western Europe, 1990–2007 (Aebi & Linde, 2012b)

In this book chapter, Aebi and Linde (2012b) deepened their analyses of crime trends in Western Europe from 1990 to 2007 by combining three types of official statistics: police-recorded offenses, suspected offenders known to police, and persons convicted. The trends and explanations are logically the same presented in their previous works (Aebi & Linde, 2010, 2012a), as the relevance of the chapter relies on the analysis of the interactions between the crime measures studied. In that perspective, police and conviction statistics showed similar overall trends, with some minor divergences in later years. Certainty of arrest (ratio of suspected offenders to recorded offenses) increased for homicide, robbery, and drug offenses but remained stable for other crimes. Certainty of conviction (ratio of persons convicted to suspected offenders) decreased for most offenses except homicide.

---

[4] https://www.euronews.com/health/2023/06/30/so-long-dry-january-which-country-drinks-the-most-alcohol-in-europe

[5] https://www.ips-journal.eu/regions/europe/gangs-of-the-north-3915/

[6] https://www.nsfk.org/news/nordic-youths-involvement-in-street-gangs/

[7] https://eucpn.org/sites/default/files/document/files/2206_Toolbox%20FR_LR.pdf (EUCPN, 2022).

Is There a Relationship Between Imprisonment and Crime in Western Europe? (Aebi et al., 2015)

Extending the analyses both in terms of the crime indicators taken into consideration and the time span covered, Aebi et al. (2015) studied the relationship between imprisonment and crime trends in Western Europe from 1982 to 2011. They found that prison population rates (stock) increased from the 1980s to 2005, then stabilized until 2011; conversely, annual entries into prisons (flow) decreased almost continuously since 1987. This apparent paradox is explained by a steady increase in the average length of detention. The composition of prison populations changed, with decreases in prisoners serving sentences for property offenses, but increases in those serving sentences for violent and drug offenses. These trends in prison populations mirrored trends in police and conviction statistics: Property crime decreased since the early 1990s; violent crime increased until the mid-2000s, then stabilized; meanwhile, drug offenses increased throughout the 1990s and 2000s.

The authors conclude there is a relationship between crime trends and imprisonment in Western Europe, with the evolution of crime affecting imprisonment rates. However, they found no evidence that increased imprisonment had a deterrent effect on violent or drug crime. They argue these findings challenge theories that view property crime as the main driver of overall crime rates, as well as claims about the deterrent effects of imprisonment. The results suggest the need to consider crime trends when analyzing changes in imprisonment rates across time and jurisdictions.

The Persistence of Lifestyles: Rates and Correlates of Homicide in Western Europe from 1960 to 2010 (Aebi & Linde, 2014)

In their following paper, Aebi and Linde (2014) focused specifically on homicide trends in 15 Western European countries over a 50-year period. They found that homicide rates increased from the mid-1960s to the early 1990s and then decreased until 2010. Both male and female victimization rates followed similar trends, with rates for males being approximately twice as high as those for females. The majority of victims were in the 30–44 age group, which contrasts with other regions of the world where victims are typically younger. Additionally, rates of infanticide (victims aged 0–14) decreased throughout the period.

Interestingly, traditional demographic and socioeconomic predictors of homicide were not significantly correlated with homicide rates or trends. Aebi and Linde (2014) proposed an explanation based on lifestyle changes since the 1960s, including increased time spent in public spaces, later marriage ages, and changes in leisure activities which contributed to the rise of homicides. They suggested that the development of "mass private property" (e.g., shopping malls) and the internet in the

1990s have contributed to the subsequent decline in homicide by altering lifestyles and routine activities.

This paper was relevant in challenging explanations of the rise of homicide between the 1960s and the 1990s that suggested a period of "decivilization in the 1960s" (Pinker, 2011) or followed Max Weber's models of conduct of life by putting the accent on the interactions of young men in public spaces (Eisner, 2008). Aebi and Linde (2014) viewed the impact of the internet as one of several factors that altered routine activities and time spent in public spaces. The authors conclude that explanations of homicide trends in Western Europe must account for changes affecting multiple age groups and both genders.

Crime Drop or Police Recording Flop? On the Relationship Between the Decrease of Offline Crime and the Increase of Online and Hybrid Crimes (Caneppele & Aebi, 2017/2019)

Realizing that the role of the cyberspace on crime trends at the international level continued to be ignored or denied—as it is respectively the case in the narratives that will be presented in the next two sections—Aebi and Caneppele (2017/2019) dedicated a paper to examine the relationship between the decline in traditional (offline) crimes and the evolution of cybercrime in Western industrialized countries. The authors argued that the "crime drop" observed since the 1990s is limited to certain traditional offline crimes, particularly property crimes and homicide, while cybercrime in the form of online and hybrid offenses has increased substantially since the 1990s.

Caneppele and Aebi (2017/2019) proposed that the rise of online and hybrid crimes has likely contributed to the drop in offline crimes by shifting criminal opportunities to the digital realm. They argued that police statistics have failed to adapt to measuring cybercrime, creating a "police recording flop" that obscures its true prevalence. In fact, victimization surveys in England and Wales suggest cybercrime may currently represent between one-third and half of all crime.

This work highlighted the limitations of traditional crime measures in capturing the realities of crime in the digital age. The authors proposed a tripartite classification of offline, online, and hybrid crimes to better reflect the current crime landscape. Caneppele and Aebi (2017/2019) concluded that the development of the cyberspace has fundamentally altered criminal opportunities and routine activities, opening a breach—in the sense proposed by Killias (2006)—in traditional crime prevention strategies. This new scenario has consolidated the private security market and led to strategic data collection by companies that could be useful to study cybercrime.

Comparative Criminology in the Digital Society (Linde & Aebi, 2020)

This paper represents the most recent evolution of the Lausanne School's thinking on international crime trends. Linde and Aebi (2020) argue that the digitalization of society marks a profound transformation that extends far beyond the scope of nineteenth-century modernization, impacting societies on a global scale. They trace the origins of the digital revolution to the computerization efforts of the 1950s, which gained significant momentum with the video games in the 1980s and the advent of the internet in the 1990s and was further accelerated by the proliferation of smartphones starting in 2007. By 2017, the ubiquity of digital technology was evident, with more global mobile phone subscriptions than habitants of the planet (103 subscriptions per 100 inhabitants).

The authors highlight several challenges that digitalization poses for criminology: (a) the need to rethink criminological theories, research methodologies, and units of analysis to incorporate the realities of cyberspace; (b) the importance of adapting units of observation to include cyberspace alongside traditional geographic units; (c) the need to include online and hybrid offenses in discussions of crime trends and cross-national comparisons; (d) the importance of updating crime measurement instruments to better capture the nuances of digital society; and (e) the need for developing new theoretical approaches and critically reassessing existing theories. Regarding the latter, Linde and Aebi (2020) consider that modernization and world systems theories appear relatively outdated for understanding cybercrime trends. In contrast, the ecological opportunities (situational) approach and civilization process theory show more promise but still require significant updates to remain relevant. They point out the hateful comments often found online, which casts doubts about the real level of *civilization* acquired and the fragility of it, which was already foreseen by Elias ([1939]/2000).

Linde and Aebi (2020) conclude that digitalization indeed entails a *paradigm shift* that requires substantial changes in comparative criminology research. This shift involves integrating cyberspace into traditional frameworks, incorporating new forms of crime into analysis, and evolving theoretical models to better understand, prevent, and respond to crime in our contemporary hybrid world.

Summary of the Contribution of the Lausanne School

In sum, the Lausanne School's body of work has consistently highlighted the complexity and regional variability of crime patterns, challenging simplistic narratives of a general "international crime drop." Their key contributions include (a) emphasizing the role of routine activities and opportunity structures in shaping crime trends; (b) highlighting the influence of significant sociopolitical changes, such as the fall of the Iron Curtain, on criminal opportunities; (c) recognizing the early impact of technological advancements, particularly the internet, on criminal behavior; and (d) proposing multifactorial explanations that consider the interplay of social, economic, and technological factors.

The work of the Lausanne School is frequently cited and has gained considerable recognition in the field of criminology. However, their persistent emphasis on the lack of uniformity in the crime drop—the absence of a "general" crime drop across all offense types and regions—is often overlooked in broader discussions. This oversight may stem from the fact that their findings contradict the narrative of a universal decline in offline crime, a phenomenon clearly observed in the United States and the United Kingdom but not necessarily replicated in continental Europe.

This selective reception of the Lausanne School's work highlights a broader issue in criminology: the tendency to generalize findings from dominant research contexts—specifically the Anglo-American sphere—to other regions without sufficient critical examination. It underscores the need for a more nuanced, context-sensitive approach to understanding global crime trends.

The *Crime and Justice* Narrative

The *Crime and Justice* narrative takes its name from the homonymous annual review of research edited by Michael Tonry since 1971. Tonry, the most international of all the US researchers, is the only person to have been president of both the American Society of Criminology and the European Society of Criminology. Now retired, he has been professor at the Universities of Minnesota, USA, and Cambridge, UK, and from 2000 to 2010, he served as the founding editor of *Criminology in Europe*, the newsletter of the European Society of Criminology. Throughout his career, Tonry often established networks of experts capable of collecting and analyzing crime data in different countries and providing meaningful explanations for the observed results. Many of the volumes of *Crime and Justice* are thematic, covering specific topics with papers written by members of these networks, and featuring introductions by Tonry, often co-authored with contributors to the same issue. These introductions provide clear and meaningful summaries of the content. The volumes are meticulously prepared through a rigorous process involving an Editorial Board, specialist guest co-editors, and conferences where draft manuscripts are discussed by authors and qualified scholars.

Crime and Justice published two volumes on international crime trends from the 1980s to the 2010s. Volume 33, titled *Crime and Punishment in Western Countries, 1980–1999*, was published in 2005 (Tonry & Farrington, 2005a); volume 43, titled *Why Crime Rates Fall, and Why They Don't*, was published in 2014 (Tonry, 2014a). Additionally, in 2010, Tonry compiled six short articles by different authors and published them in issue 9/1 of the ESC Newsletter as a special feature under the title *Why are crime rates falling (or are they)?* (Tonry, 2010). In the *Crime and Justice* narrative, trends in online and hybrid offenses (Caneppele and Aebi, 2017/2019) are not mentioned.

Crime and Punishment in Western Countries, 1980–1999 (Tonry & Farrington, 2005a)

This book, published in 2005 as volume 33 of *Crime and Justice*, represents a significant contribution to the study of contemporary international crime trends namely because of its rigorous methodology. It includes 11 articles and is the result of a conference held in Cambridge in 1999. The 6-year lag between the conference and the publication highlights the extensive efforts involved in completing it.

Tonry and Farrington's (2005b) introductory article presents a sophisticated comparative study of crime rates and trends across eight countries: Australia, Canada, England and Wales, Netherlands, Switzerland, Scotland, Sweden, and the United States. The study aimed to standardize crime and punishment data to facilitate meaningful cross-national comparisons, focusing on six offenses—residential burglary, vehicle theft, robbery, serious assault, rape, and homicide—over the years 1980 to 1999. For each country, the authors of the articles included in the book collected data on various stages of the criminal justice process for these offenses, including the number of crimes committed (estimated via national victimization surveys), reported to the police, recorded by the police, offenders convicted, offenders sentenced to custody, average sentence length, and average time served. They then compared these quantities with the national populations and estimated linking probabilities, such as the likelihood of an offender being convicted, or a convicted person being sentenced to custody. Tonry and Farrington (2005b) do not introduce the concept of a general "international crime drop" because the data collected do not support such a hypothesis.

Their main findings are that (a) burglary rates rose in the 1980s but decreased in most countries from the early 1990s onward; (b) robbery rates showed no clear trend in most countries, with increases in England and Scotland and decreases in the United States; (c) homicide rates either fell substantially toward the end of the twentieth century or remained flat at low levels; and (d) motor vehicle theft rates fell in most countries during the 1990s and in several during the 1980s.

The authors note that the results for these offenses align with data from the *International Crime Victim Survey (ICVS)* (van Kesteren et al., 2000) and the *European Sourcebook of Crime and Criminal Justice Statistics* for homicide, burglary, and motor vehicle theft but show mixed patterns for robbery (CoE, 1999). On the contrary, Tonry and Farrington (2005b) express skepticism about trends in assault, rape, and robbery, noting that increases in the official data collected for these crimes may reflect changes in reporting and recording practices rather than actual increases in violence. This skepticism toward the rise of nonlethal violent offenses becomes a recurring theme in the *Crime and Justice* narrative. To support their explanation based on the declining tolerance of violence in Western societies, Tonry and Farrington (2005b) quote Blumstein and Beck (1999) who worked with US data only. Furthermore, they do not analyze trends in the levels of reporting rates as recorded by victimization surveys which, if their hypothesis was correct, should have been increasing. The analyses of the ICVS data conducted years later by Aebi and Linde (2010, 2012a) showed that at that time, the percentages of violent victimizations reported by the victims to the police were not increasing.

In addition, Tonry and Farrington (2005b) state that "Because the most reliable crime counts are for homicide, and assault and robbery rates should be probabilistically related to homicide rates, there is reason to be skeptical that the official data reported in the [European] Sourcebook reflect reality. Accordingly, we believe that no conclusions about true crime trends can be drawn from Sourcebook data about recorded rates of rape, robbery, and assault" (Tonry & Farrington, 2005b: 13). This notion of a correlation between homicide and other nonlethal crimes is deeply rooted in American criminological thought, but does not seem to hold universally, especially in continental Western Europe (Aebi & Linde, 2016). This perspective overlooks important factors such as improvements in medical healthcare, which have contributed to a decrease in completed homicides while attempted homicides have increased (Linde, 2018). In many European countries, the distinction between attempted and completed homicides is crucial, and relying solely on completed homicides—as is common in the United States, where they are categorized as murder—can lead to skewed interpretations of crime trends.

Why Crime Rates Are Falling Throughout the Western World (Tonry, 2014a)

This book, published as volume 43 of *Crime and Justice*, includes eight articles and is the result of a conference held in Bologna in 2012. It arrived at a moment when the notion of an "international crime drop" had been taken for granted by many criminologists.

Tonry's (2014b) introductory article, however, strikes a cautionary note. While agreeing that homicide and property crime have declined substantially since the 1990s across the developed world, he argues trends in other violent crimes were more complex and ambiguous. Tonry accepts the evidence of homicide declines as definitive. Homicide is the most reliably measured crime, with health statistics on deaths corroborating the police data showing steep drops in all Western countries starting in the early to mid-1990s, after increases in the preceding decades. Property crime has also clearly fallen based on both police records and victimization surveys.

Tonry (2014b) contends that for assault, robbery, rape, and nonlethal violent offenses in general, the picture is murkier. Police records show decreases in the English-speaking countries and parts of continental Europe since the 1990s but increases in some other European countries. Victimization surveys in several countries, especially in Scandinavia, also point to rising violence. Tonry (2014b) attributes these seeming contradictions not to real differences in violence trends but to changes in reporting and recording. According to him, victims have become more likely over time to report incidents to police, but at different rates across countries. Police have also shifted to recording more reported incidents as crimes, sometimes due to policy changes to be more victim-oriented. In addition, cultural thresholds of tolerance for violence, especially domestic and sexual, have fallen, leading more people to define incidents as crimes. These changes in reporting, recording, and cultural meanings have inflated official rates of violent crime to varying degrees in different countries at different times, Tonry argues. He suggests violence has likely fallen everywhere but this is obscured in some official data, especially in continental Europe, that may lag behind the United States and United Kingdom in the timing of these artifact effects.

In terms of explanations of these trends, while agreeing that security improvements seem a likely cause of property crime declines, Tonry (2014b) is more skeptical that they explain violence trends given the apparent divergences. He instead favors theories focused on evolving cultural thresholds and social controls, building on insights from Durkheim, Elias, and others about the "civilizing process" that has reduced violence over the centuries. Recent declines are seen as a resumption of this long-term trend after a 1960s–1980s disruption from rapid social change.

In short, Tonry (2014b) supports the idea of a general crime drop in Western highly industrialized societies. The evidence is overwhelming that homicide and property crime have fallen in these societies, but for other violent crimes, official records are misleading. Nevertheless, underneath the apparent divergences, violence is probably declining everywhere, he concludes, driven primarily by long-term cultural shifts.

Tonry's (2014b) analysis of available data aligns with much research indicating that nonlethal violent offenses did not universally decline in continental Europe, unlike the trends observed in homicide and property crime. This divergence is significant as some narratives overlook these contrasting trends (see Farrell et al., 2014, in the next section). While we share the perspective on heightened sensitivity to violence in these countries, we have a difference of opinion regarding the extent of its influence. For increased reporting to fully explain the rising police-recorded and conviction rates, it would have needed to grow consistently and at a significant pace year after year (Aebi & Linde, 2012a). Moreover, victimization surveys do not reflect this major reporting increase, which further complicates this explanation (Aebi & Linde, 2010, 2012a). Accepting that violence is declining, contrary to what official data suggest, requires a leap of faith that we are not willing to take. Additionally, if the assumption is that violence is not increasing despite the empirical evidence, it raises the question of why it should be considered declining rather than stable.

We concur with Tonry (2014b) regarding the role of situational crime prevention in reducing property offenses, a view that we have been holding since our early works on crime trends (Killias & Aebi, 2000a; Aebi, 2004a, b). Regarding the decline in homicide rates since the late Middle Ages, the perspective on the impact of Elias' civilizing process is shared too. However, in the short term, we consider that lifestyle changes explain better the increase in homicide from the 1960s to the 1990s and its subsequent decrease (Aebi & Linde, 2014). This decrease is linked to the increase in time spent in virtual environments, beginning with video games in the 1980s, accelerating with the expansion of the internet in the 1990s, and further propelled by the advent of smartphones from 2007 onward (Linde & Aebi, 2020). In this context, we acknowledge that choosing between a cultural and a lifestyle explanation with the available data is largely a matter of interpretation.

In sum, while Tonry (2014b) rightly highlights the complexity of violence trends, his suggestion that they are universally falling is not fully supported by the evidence. Alternate multifactor explanations, such as the ones developed by researchers from the Lausanne school and presented in the previous section, may provide a more compelling account of European crime trends, although this remains open to debate.

The Security Hypothesis Narrative

The narrative of the security hypothesis references an impressive number of articles written by Graham Farrell with various co-authors, usually including the term "crime drop" in their titles.[8] In the empirical sections of these articles, Farrell and colleagues frequently analyze data from the United States, Canada, the United Kingdom, Australia, and New Zealand—English-speaking and common-law countries where there is consensus about a general decrease in offline crimes in the 1990s and 2000s. They conclude that this crime drop can only be explained through a security hypothesis inspired by the routine activities approach. Furthermore, based on an analysis of data from the ICVS, they argue that there is an international crime drop, which can only be explained through their security hypothesis. Notably, Farrell and his colleagues arrived relatively late to the crime trends debate—their first article in a newsletter is from 2008—and they prefer to ignore previous explanations based on opportunity-based theories, such as those provided by Killias and Aebi (2000a) and Aebi (2004a, b), proclaiming systematically that they were the first to propose such an explanation.

As Farrell and colleagues' security hypothesis has been extensively presented in several of their papers, we have selected the one we consider the most comprehensive for summarizing it here (Farrell et al., 2014). This paper, included in the already mentioned volume 43 of *Crime and Justice*, makes a compelling case that security improvements are the most likely explanation for the widespread drops in crime experienced in many developed countries since the early 1990s. The authors argue that most other prominent hypotheses fail to adequately account for key features of the international crime declines. In particular, they apply four key tests to assess the viability of different explanations.

First, can the hypothesis be applied to multiple countries that experienced crime drops? Many explanations developed in the US context, such as changes in abortion laws or policing strategies, do not fit the international nature of the crime declines.

---

[8] See in particular Farrell et al. (2008, 2010, 2011, 2014, 2015) and Farrell and Birks (2018, 2020).

Second, is the hypothesis consistent with the fact that crime was increasing for several decades prior to the 1990s? Some explanations, like the civilizing process or lead poisoning, imply a long-term downward trend at odds with earlier increases.

Third, can the hypothesis account for increases in some crimes, like phone theft and e-crimes, while most crimes dropped? Demographic shifts or waning drug markets, for instance, would predict broad declines across all crime types.

Fourth, is the hypothesis compatible with variation in the timing and trajectory of crime drops across countries and crime types? Imprisonment rates or economic factors varied too much internationally to explain the common overall pattern.

Of 17 hypotheses examined, Farrell et al. (2014) consider that 16 fail one or more of these tests. Unsurprisingly, their security hypothesis is the only one that passes all four. The strongest evidence would come from the auto theft declines. Multiple studies across different countries point to improved vehicle security in the form of electronic immobilizers and central locking as driving the dramatic falls in car theft. The spread of these measures aligns closely with the timing of the theft reductions in the United States, the United Kingdom, Australia, and the Netherlands. Mounting evidence also suggests household burglary fell due to better security, such as stronger door and window locks and security lighting.

Farrell et al. (2014) then intend to explain the crime drop—which for them is general, in the sense that it includes all kinds of offline offenses, and international. Unsurprisingly, they face a difficult challenge when trying to explain a decrease in violent offenses through a hypothesis that the Lausanne School had been applying for years to explain the decline of offline property offenses (see the previous sections).

According to Farrell et al. (2014), as offenders found it harder to steal cars and break into homes, this may have had a knock-on effect in reducing other street crimes and violence. They also state that most offenders are generalists, and property crimes dominate the criminal career, frequently preceding violent offenses. Hence, Farrell et al. (2014) propose two keyways in which security improvements likely reduced violence:

1. The keystone hypothesis: Reducing car theft denied offenders a means to travel to commit other crimes. Disrupting this key crime type undercut the general criminal career.
2. The debut crime hypothesis: Making adolescent offending like joyriding harder delayed the onset of criminal careers, leading to fewer offenders progressing to chronic offending.

In summary, in line with the explanations of the Lausanne School (see the previous sections), the preponderance of evidence indicates security improvements are the most compelling explanation that fits the international decline of property offenses. Whether this may have had an indirect effect on violent offenses, as proposed by Farrell et al. (2014), is a matter of debate. While further research on other crime types is still needed, the security hypothesis provides a convincing and parsimonious account of the drop in offline property offenses compared to rival theories.

It suggests that designing out crime opportunities may have far-reaching benefits in reducing offending.

A major difference between the Lausanne School and the security hypothesis narratives is that for the latter, the crime drop concerns all offenses. Interestingly, confronted with the same ICVS data for the few countries that participated five times, Farrell et al. (2014) and Aebi and Linde (2010, 2012a) reached different conclusions regarding trends in violent offenses. It is worth noting that Tonry and Farrington (2005b) had already warned about the limitations of the ICVS for establishing crime trends due to the sample sizes, typically about 2000 per country, and nonresponse rates, typically 30–50%.

Furthermore, there are several clashes between research conducted by both groups and the way in which the works of the Lausanne School are presented by Farrell and colleagues in most of their articles. The latter primarily concentrate on the United Kingdom, Australia, and the United States, potentially overlooking important variations in crime trends across other countries, particularly in continental Europe. Farrell et al. (2014) mischaracterized Aebi and Linde's (2012b) findings, claiming they suggested no "general" crime drop in Europe due to variation between countries. In reality, Aebi and Linde's work presented a more nuanced view, showing varied trends for different types of offenses (see the previous sections).

Additionally, Farrell et al. (2014) rejected the "internet hypothesis"—i.e., the role of cyberspace in explaining crime trends—without fully considering its complexities or acknowledging prior peer-reviewed studies on the topic, such as Aebi and Linde (2010). Similarly, Farrell and Birks (2018) dismissed attempts to correlate the rise of online and hybrid crimes with the decline of certain offline crimes (Caneppele & Aebi, 2019/17), arguing that "the causal mechanisms are wrong." This approach may overlook the complex, process-based nature of societal changes and their impact on crime. To conclude, Farrell et al. (2014) claim originality for applying routine activity theory to crime trends, despite earlier work by researchers from the Lausanne school (e.g., Killias & Aebi, 2000a, Aebi, 2004a, b) that had already applied opportunity-based theories to European crime trends.

In fact, the insistence of Farrell and colleagues on the concept of an "international crime drop" may be an overgeneralization, especially when applied to Europe as a whole, given the lack of comprehensive data for many countries and the significant historical events affecting crime statistics in Central and Eastern Europe. Finally, while criticizing others for relying on official statistics, Farrell et al. (2014) do not fully acknowledge the limitations of victimization surveys, especially in cross-national and long-term comparisons.

Discussion and Conclusion

The debate surrounding the so-called "international crime drop" has been a major topic in criminology for the past three decades. This review has traced the evolution of this concept from its origins in the United States to its broader application in international contexts. Through an examination of four major narratives—the all-American, the Lausanne School, the *Crime and Justice*, and the security hypothesis—we have highlighted the complexities and nuances of interpreting crime trends across different countries and crime types.

Several key points emerge from this review:

1. The complexity of crime trends: The notion of a general "international crime drop" is an oversimplification. While there is evidence of declining rates for certain types of crime (particularly property crimes and homicide) in many Western countries since the 1990s, trends in other violent crimes have been more variable, especially in continental Europe.
2. Methodological Challenges: Cross-national comparisons of crime trends face significant methodological hurdles, including differences in legal definitions, reporting practices, and data collection methods. The debate highlights the importance of using multiple data sources, including both official statistics and victimization surveys, to gain a more comprehensive picture.
3. Divergent explanations: While there is general agreement on the decline of property crimes and homicide in many Western countries, explanations for these trends vary. Opportunity-based theories—supported by the three international perspectives—has gained traction in explaining property crime declines, but their application to violent crime trends is more contentious.
4. The role of technology: The impact of technological changes, particularly the rise of the internet and smartphones, on crime trends has been a point of contention. While some researchers (notably the Lausanne School) have emphasized its importance, others have been more skeptical or have overlooked its potential influence.
5. Regional variations: The review highlights significant differences between trends observed in English-speaking countries (particularly the United States and United Kingdom) and those in continental Europe. This underscores the need for context-specific analyses that consider unique historical, social, and cultural factors.
6. The emergence of Cybercrime: The rise of online and hybrid offenses has been largely overlooked in many analyses of the crime drop, potentially skewing our understanding of overall crime trends.
7. Theoretical implications: The debate has challenged existing criminological theories and highlighted the need for more dynamic, multifactor explanations that can account for variations across crime types, regions, and time periods.

These findings have several implications for criminology and criminal justice policy:

1. A need for nuanced analysis: Future research on crime trends should avoid overgeneralization and strive for more nuanced, context-sensitive analyses that consider variations across different types of offenses, geographical regions, and time periods.

2. Improving data collection: There is a pressing need to develop more sophisticated methods for measuring and analyzing cybercrime to ensure a comprehensive understanding of contemporary crime patterns.
3. Theoretical development: The field would benefit from the development of more integrated theoretical approaches that can account for the complex interplay of factors influencing crime trends, including technological changes, socioeconomic factors, and cultural shifts.
4. Policy Implications: While improved security measures appear to have been effective in reducing property crimes, their impact on violent crime is less clear. Policymakers should consider a range of approaches when addressing different types of criminal behavior.
5. International cooperation: Given the global nature of many contemporary crime issues, particularly cybercrime, there is a need for increased international cooperation in both research and policy development.

In conclusion, while the concept of an "international crime drop" has stimulated valuable research and debate, it has also highlighted the risks of oversimplifying complex social phenomena. Future research should remain open to diverse perspectives and methodologies, critically examine underlying assumptions, and strive for a more nuanced understanding of crime trends that reflects the complexities of our increasingly interconnected and hybrid world.

References

Aebi, M. F. (Guest Editor). (2004). Special double issue on crime trends in Western and Eastern European countries. *European Journal on Criminal Policy and Research, 10*(2–3), 105–253.

Aebi, M. F. (2004a). Crime trends in Europe from 1990 to 2000. In K. Aromaa & S. Nevala (Eds.), *Crime and crime control in an integrating Europe: Plenary presentations held at the third annual conference of the European Society of Criminology, Helsinki 2003* (HEUNI Publication Series No. 44) (pp. 39–60). HEUNI. http://www.heuni.fi/uploads/ob35f37b1qqdnk(1).pdf

Aebi, M. F. (2004b). Crime trends in Western Europe from 1990 to 2000. *European Journal on Criminal Policy and Research, 10*(2–3), 163–186. https://doi.org/10.1007/s10610-004-3412-1

Aebi, M. F. & Jehle, J. -M. (Guest Editors). (2018). Special issue on crime and criminal justice in Europe. *European Journal on Criminal Policy and Research, 24*(1), 1–119.

Aebi, M. F., & Linde, A. (2010). Is there a crime drop in Western Europe? *European Journal on Criminal Policy and Research, 16*(4), 251–277. https://doi.org/10.1007/s10610-010-9130-y

Aebi, M. F., & Linde, A. (2012a). Conviction statistics as an indicator of crime trends in Europe from 1990 to 2006. *European Journal on Criminal Policy and Research, 18*(1), 103–144. https://doi.org/10.1007/s10610-011-9166-7

Aebi, M. F., & Linde, A. (2012b). Crime trends in Western Europe according to official statistics from 1990 to 2007. In J. van Dijk, A. Tseloni, & G. Farrell (Eds.), *The international crime drop: New directions in research* (pp. 37–75). Palgrave Macmillan UK.

Aebi, M. F., & Linde, A. (2014). The persistence of lifestyles: Rates and correlates of homicide in Western Europe from 1960 to 2010. *European Journal of Criminology, 11*(5), 552–577. https://doi.org/10.1177/1477370814541178

Aebi, M. F., & Linde, A. (2016). Long-term trends in crime: Continuity and change. In P. Knepper & A. Johansen (Eds.), *The Oxford Handbook of the history of crime and criminal justice* (pp. 57–87). Oxford University Press.

Aebi, M. F., Aromaa, K., Aubusson de Cavarlay, B., Barclay, G., Gruszczynska, B., von Hofer, H., et al. (2006). *European sourcebook of crime and criminal justice statistics – 2006* (3rd ed.). Boom Juridische Uitgevers.

Aebi, M. F., Aubusson de Cavarlay, B., Barclay, G., Gruszczynska, B., Harrendorf, S., Heiskanen, M., et al. (2010). *European sourcebook of crime and criminal justice statistics – 2010* (4th ed.). Boom Juridische Uitgevers.

Aebi, M. F., Akdeniz, G., Barclay, G., Campistol, C., Caneppele, S., Gruszczynska, B., et al. (2014). *European sourcebook of crime and criminal justice statistics 2014* (5th ed.). European Institute for Crime Prevention and Control, affiliated with the United Nations (HEUNI).

Aebi, M. F., Linde, A., & Delgrande, N. (2015). Is there a relationship between imprisonment and crime in Western Europe? *European Journal on Criminal Policy and Research, 21*(3), 425–446. https://doi.org/10.1007/s10610-015-9274-x

Aebi, M. F., Berger-Kolopp, L., Burkhardt, C., & Tiago, M. M. (2019a). *Prisons in Europe: 2005–2015. Volume 1: Country Profiles*. Council of Europe Publishing.

Aebi, M. F., Berger-Kolopp, L., Burkhardt, C., & Tiago, M. M. (2019b). *Prisons in Europe: 2005–2015. Volume 2: Sourcebook of prison statistics*. Council of Europe Publishing.

Aebi, M. F., Berger-Kolopp, L., Burkhardt, C., Chopin, J., Hashimoto, Y. Z., & Tiago, M. M. (2019c). *Foreign offenders in prison and on probation in Europe: Trends from 2005 to 2015 (inmates) and situation in 2015 (inmates and probationers)*. Council of Europe Publishing.

Aebi, M. F., Caneppele, S., Harrendorf, S., Hashimoto, Y. Z., Jehle, J.-M., Khan, T. S., Kühn, O., Lewis, C., Molnar, L., Smit, P., & Þórisdóttir, R. (2021). *European sourcebook of crime and criminal justice statistics – 2021* (6th ed.). Göttingen University Press.

Aebi, M. F., Caneppele, S., Harrendorf, S., Hacin, R., Hashimoto, Y. Z., Jehle, J.-M., Kensey, A., Khan, T. S., Molnar, L., Þórisdóttir, R., & Smit, P. (2024). *European sourcebook of crime and criminal justice statistics – 2024* (7th ed.). Preliminary Publication. Université de Lausanne. Series UNILCRIM 2024/3.

Barbagli, M. (Ed.). (2000). *Perché è diminuita la criminalità negli Stati Uniti?* Il Mulino.

Baumer, E. P., Vélez, M. B., & Rosenfeld, R. (2018). Bringing crime trends back into criminology: A critical assessment of the literature and a blueprint for future inquiry. *Annual Review of Criminology, 1*(1), 39–61.

Blumstein, A., & Beck, A. J. (1999). Population growth in US prisons, 1980–1996. *Crime and Justice, 26*, 17–61.

Blumstein, A., & Wallman, J. (Eds.). (2000). *The crime drop in America*. Cambridge University Press.

Caneppele, S., & Aebi, M. F. (2019). Crime drop or police recording flop? On the relationship between the decrease of offline crime and the increase of online and hybrid crimes. *Policing: A Journal of Policy and Practice, 13*(1), 66–79. Published online on September 13, 2017.

CoE – Council of Europe. (1999). *European sourcebook of crime and criminal justice*.

Cohen, L. E., & Felson, M. (1979). Social change and crime rate trends: A routine activity approach. *American Sociological Review, 44*(4), 588–608. https://doi.org/10.2307/2094589

Dennis, N. (Ed.). (1997). *Zero tolerance: Policing a free society*. IEA Health and Welfare Unit.

Dennis, N. (Ed.). (1998). *Zero tolerance: Policing a free society. Enlarged and revised* (2nd ed.). IEA Health and Welfare Unit.

Eisner, M. (2008). Modernity strikes back? A historical perspective on the latest increase in interpersonal violence (1960–1990). *International Journal of Conflict and Violence, 2*(2), 288–316.

Elias, N. ([1939] 2000). *The civilizing process: Sociogenetic and psychogenetic investigations*. Oxford: Blackwell.

EUCPN [European Crime Prevention Network] (2022). *Toolbox on street gang prevention*. Brussels. EUCPN Toolbox Series.

Farrell, G., & Birks, D. (2018). Did cybercrime cause the crime drop? *Crime Science, 7*(1), 8.

Farrell, G., & Birks, D. (2020). Further rejection of the cybercrime hypothesis. *Crime Science, 9*(1), 4.

Farrell, G., Tilley, N., Tseloni, A., & Mailley, J. (2008). The crime drop and the security hypothesis. *Newsletter of the British Society of Criminology, 62*(March), 17–21.

Farrell, G., Tilley, N., Tseloni, A., & Mailley, J. (2010). Explaining and sustaining the crime drop: Clarifying the role of opportunity-related theories. *Crime Prevention and Community Safety, 12,* 24–41.
Farrell, G., Tseloni, A., Mailley, J., & Tilley. N. (2011). The crime drop and the security hypothesis. *Journal of Research in Crime and Delinquency, 48*(2), 147–175.
Farrell, G., Tilley, N., & Tseloni, A. (2014). Why the crime drop? *Crime and Justice, 43*(1), 421–490.
Farrell, G., Laycock, G., & Tilley, N. (2015). Debuts and legacies: The crime drop and the role of adolescence-limited and persistent offending. *Crime Science, 4*(1), 16.
Farrington, D. P., Langan, P. A., & Tonry, M. (2004). *Cross-national studies in crime and justice.* Bureau of Justice Statistics, U.S. Department of Justice.
Felson, M. (1998). *Crime and everyday life* (2nd ed.). Pine Forge Press.
Felson, M. (1999, May). *Crime rate trends and cycles: Changes in modern society.* Paper presented at the conference 'Why is Crime Diminishing in the United States'. Istituto Carlo Cattaneo.
Hindelang, M. J., Gottfredson, M. R., & Garofalo, J. (1978). *Victims of personal crime: An empirical foundation for a theory of personal victimization.* Ballinger.
Killias, M. (2006). The opening and closing of breaches. *European Journal of Criminology, 3*(1), 11–31. https://doi.org/10.1177/1477370806059079
Killias, M., & Aebi, M. F. (2000a). Crime trends in Europe from 1990 to 1996: How Europe illustrates the limits of the American experience. *European Journal on Criminal Policy and Research, 8*(1), 43–63.
Killias, M., & Aebi, M. F. (2000b). Un confronto tra gli Stati Uniti e l'Europa. In M. Barbagli (Ed.), *Perché è diminuita la criminalità negli Stati Uniti?* (pp. 239–258). Il Mulino.
Killias, M. & Jehle, J. M. (Guest Editors) (2000). Special issue on crime and criminal justice in Europe. *European Journal on Criminal Policy and Research, 8*(1), pp. 1-119.
Killias, M., Barclay, G., Smit, P., Aebi, M. F., Tavares, C., Aubusson de Cavarlay, B., et al. (2003). *European sourcebook of crime and criminal justice statistics 2003* (2nd ed.). Boom Juridische Uitgevers.
Linde, A. (2018). The impact of improvements in medical care resources on homicide trends: The case of Germany (1977–2011). *European Journal on Criminal Policy and Research, 24*(1), 99–119.
Linde, A., & Aebi, M. F. (2015). La pertinencia de la teoría de las actividades cotidianas a través del tiempo y el espacio: Un modelo multifactorial explicativo de las tendencias delictivas posteriores a la reunificación del continente europeo. In F. Miró-Linares, J. R. Agustina-Sanllehí, J. E. Medina-Sarmiento, & L. Summers (Eds.), *Crimen, oportunidad y vida diaria: Libro homenaje al Profesor Dr. Marcus Felson* (pp. 73–104). Dykinson.
Linde, A., & Aebi, M. F. (2020). La criminologie comparée à l'heure de la société numérique: Les théories traditionnelles peuvent-elles expliquer les tendances de la cyber-délinquance? *Revue Internationale de Criminologie et de Police Technique et Scientifique, 73*(4), 387–414.
Pinker, S. (2011). *The better angels of our nature: Why violence has declined.* Penguin Books.
Tonry, M. (2010). Why are crime rates falling (or are they)? *Criminology in Europe: Newsletter of the European Society of Criminology, 9*(1), 3.
Tonry, M. (Ed.). (2014a). *Crime and justice, volume 43: Why crime rates fall, and why they don't.* The University of Chicago Press.
Tonry, M. (2014b). Why crime rates are falling throughout the Western world. *Crime and Justice, 43,* 1–63.
Tonry, M., & Farrington, D. P. (2005a). *Crime and punishment in western countries, 1980–1999* (Crime and justice) (Vol. 33). University of Chicago Press.
Tonry, M., & Farrington, D. P. (2005b). Punishment and crime across space and time. *Crime and Justice, 33,* 1–39.
Travis, J. (1998). Social institutions and the crime bust of the 1990s. *Journal of Criminal Law and Criminology, 88*(4), 1173–1174. https://scholarlycommons.law.northwestern.edu/jclc/vol88/iss4/1

van Dijk, J., van Kesteren, J. N., & Smit, P. (2007). *Criminal victimisation in international perspective, key findings from the 2004–2005 ICVS and EU ICS*. Boom.
van Dijk, J., Tseloni, A., & Farrell, G. (Eds.). (2012). *The international crime drop: New directions in research*. Palgrave Macmillan.
van Kesteren, J. N., Mayhew, P., & Nieuwbeerta, P. (2000). *Criminal victimisation in seventeen industrialised countries: Key-findings from the 2000 international crime victims survey*. Boom.
Varese, F. (2011). *Mafias on the move: How organized crime conquers new territories*. Princeton University Press.
Wilson, J. Q., & Kelling, G. L. (1982). Broken windows: The police and neighborhood safety. *Atlantic Monthly, 249*(3), 29–38.
Zimring, F. E. (2007). *The great American crime decline*. Oxford University Press.

Open Access This chapter is licensed under the terms of the Creative Commons Attribution 4.0 International License (http://creativecommons.org/licenses/by/4.0/), which permits use, sharing, adaptation, distribution and reproduction in any medium or format, as long as you give appropriate credit to the original author(s) and the source, provide a link to the Creative Commons license and indicate if changes were made.

The images or other third party material in this chapter are included in the chapter's Creative Commons license, unless indicated otherwise in a credit line to the material. If material is not included in the chapter's Creative Commons license and your intended use is not permitted by statutory regulation or exceeds the permitted use, you will need to obtain permission directly from the copyright holder.

Chapter 3
Digitalization, Social Change, and Crime Trends: A Literature Review to Build a Conjecture

Fernando Miró-Llinares and Marcelo F. Aebi

What Slow and Abrupt Changes Can Have in Common

Among researchers, there is much more agreement than disagreement regarding the importance, necessity, and inherent challenges of delving into the historical analysis of crime trends. Conversely, there is much more disagreement than agreement when it comes to pinpointing the precise reasons behind shifts in these trends. The overarching goal, shared by many, of scrutinizing crime patterns across various timeframes—be it globally, nationally, or at the city level—is to uncover insights into the past and the macro-level evolution of criminal activities and then, by juxtaposing these trends with changes in a myriad of social factors, to identify explanatory variables that can elucidate micro-level shifts in crime dynamics (Rosenfeld, 2018). The imperative arises from the need to refine our understanding of crime and, consequently, enhance our ability to predict its trajectories, rationalize public policies, and optimize resource allocation related to crime prevention (Blumstein & Rosenfeld, 2008). Despite this urgency, the forward-looking aspect of this endeavor has received considerably less scholarly attention (Austin et al., 2019). The formidable challenge of uncovering explanatory factors behind trends rests on several well-acknowledged barriers. These barriers are often categorized into issues related to access to data—whether due to data unavailability or inaccessibility (Hebenton & Jou, 2018) or to their validity (Aebi & Linde, 2016)—and challenges in comprehending and interpreting the complex social conditions that impact crime rates

F. Miró-Llinares (✉)
Crimina Center, University Miguel Hernández of Elche, Elche, Spain
e-mail: f.miro@crimina.es

M. F. Aebi
School of Criminal Sciences, Faculty of Law, Criminal Sciences and Public Administration, University of Lausanne, Lausanne, Switzerland
e-mail: marcelo.aebi@unil.ch

© The Author(s) 2025
M. F. Aebi et al. (eds.), *Understanding Crime Trends in a Hybrid Society*, SpringerBriefs in Criminology, https://doi.org/10.1007/978-3-031-72387-2_3

(Rosenfeld & Weisburd, 2016), including chronocentrism, parochialism, and causationism (Aebi & Linde, 2016).

Perhaps this explains why, although the study of crime trends is as old as criminology itself, it is usually complex to identify the factors that affect the change in crime rates over time (Aebi & Linde, 2016; Rosenfeld & Weisburd, 2016), and it is much more common to find in the literature on the analysis of a specific crime trend significant disagreements about the causes than essential agreements on the reason for the change. There are always exceptions however. In fact, of the last two trends that have been of special academic interest, one of them complies with the rule, since there is a clear disagreement in the diagnosis of the reasons for such a change in trend, while the other seems an exception, as it has led to an apparent general consensus on the explanations for it. The first one is the offline crime drop in America; the second one is the crime drop during the pandemic-related lockdowns.

The first one is the debate about the so-called "crime drop," which occupied the first two chapters of this book. In order to simplify the discussion, the debate about trends in violent offenses in Europe treated in the previous chapter will be left aside, and this chapter will concentrate only in the explanations provided for the decrease of homicides and property offenses in Europe as well as the general decrease of offline offenses in the United States. In that context, what has given rise to more literature and more disagreement has been the identification of potential explanations for this change in trend. It is true that there is a more or less generalized agreement that the offline crime drop would involve a set of decreases in different types of criminal behaviors from different cohorts that could be due to a confluence of causes rather than a single condition causing the overall decrease (Aebi & Linde, 2010; Blumstein & Farrington, 2000; Van Dijk & Tseloni, 2012; Zimring, 2006; Kim et al., 2016). But beyond that, and from the very beginning of the discussion, there have been many and very different explanations that have been offered for the change in trend. Reasons related to a deeper change that would have to do with the "long duree" such as the process of civilization (Elias & Hammer, 1939) that has been experienced in the last century and that would have led to a decrease in crime only interrupted by the rise in the 1960s and 1970s (Pinker, 2011; Eisner, 2008; Aebi & Linde, 2014). Demographic and political changes of various types that would have had a slower and harder to perceive impact have also been mentioned, such as the role of institutions in attitudes toward them and toward specific types of crimes, or the political and economic context itself (Farrall, 2017). And within these latter factors is where some of the changes that have been cited as totally or partially determinant of the crime drop should be framed, such as changes in the environments of criminal opportunity due to technological modifications that would have improved surveillance and reduced criminal opportunities (Farrell et al., 2011), as well as more indirect changes in lifestyles that would have increased time spent at home and reduced time on the streets, and with it also some opportunities for traditional crime (Aebi & Linde, 2010; Miró-Llinares & Moneva, 2019). In this perspective, only Aebi and Linde (2010, 2012a, b; 2014; Linde & Aebi, 2020) have been insisting since they started writing together on crime trends on the role of time spent on the internet on lifestyles and how this affected these trends.

As anticipated, there is less divergence regarding the origin of the other crime decline trend, albeit soon reversed, that has been the subject of special attention from criminology, focusing on crime rates during the Covid-19 crisis. A quick look at the initial works that have analyzed the impact of the Covid-19 crisis on different forms of crime in various countries (which will be expanded upon later) shows us that almost all studies agree in placing changes in mobility as the reason behind the change in trends, and even behind some increases such as domestic-related crime (Piquero et al., 2020), and cybercrime (Buil-Gil et al., 2020; Kemp et al., 2021; Johnson & Nikolovska, 2022; Miró-Llinares, 2021) as well as their impact on prison populations (Aebi & Tiago, 2020a, b). Based on the premises of criminal opportunity, it seems that the reduction in everyday activities in the streets and in other public places during the harsh moments of confinement would explain the generalized decreases in crime during those periods, and the increases in those crimes whose opportunities are generated by spending more time at home (Payne & Morgan, 2020). In addition, the different degrees of confinement and the prohibitions of activity imposed by governmental institutions would explain the different evolution of crime (Payne et al., 2020; Mohler et al., 2020), which ties even more clearly the development of trends with the different ways in which mobility was affected and, thus, the convergence between aggressors and potential victims.

It should not surprise us that, on one hand, there is clear agreement on the origin of the Covid trend and that, on the other, there is a profound disagreement regarding the offline crime drop. The reason, using Braudel (1958) again, does not have to be the different nature of the causes of change, but the different "clock" at which they might be moving, even if they were related. While one trend, the one related to Covid-19, is happening at a faster speed due to the appearance of an event that abruptly modifies social conditions determinant of violent behavior, such as mobility and its incidence on the convergence between aggressors and victims, the other moves much more slowly, at the speed at which social changes occur for demographic or technological reasons. Something similar to this has been suggested by Rosenfeld when he talks about the study of crime trends moving between what he calls "normal science," the study of slow changes in crime over time in relation to also gradual changes in criminal opportunities or sanctions, and exogenous shocks, about the study of unexpected and abrupt changes in crime rates caused by also abrupt and unforeseen exogenous shocks that would not be explainable according to the assumptions of normal science and would require new explanatory approaches (Rosenfeld, 2018). But exogenous changes and slow changes can coincide at a certain moment, when in the middle of a certain slow trend of modification of crime rates due to demographic, technological, or other reasons, and specific events occur that create new trends. In these cases, it is advisable not to confuse the effects due to the eventual change with those that have to do with the conjunctural change. And it is also important to keep in mind that, while the causes of one and the other may be different, they can also be related, albeit at different paces.

This chapter addresses the issue of the role that the process of digitalization, which started more than three decades ago (Kotkin, 2002), could have played, and will play in the future, on crime trends. It does so, moreover, by expressly adopting a scientific attitude that, following the beautiful and simplifying idea of Isaiah Berlin (1953), would be far from that of the Hedgehog, and aspires to be that of the fox, less absorbed in fixed ideas that are already known and more attentive to those that are not, to explore new possibilities. In this sense, the objective of the work is the theoretical construction of the conjecture that in the crime trends of the last decades, this process of digitalization has played a role, starting from overcoming some misconceptions that have arisen about these trends and their possible causal relationships. While some effects had already been noticed and were undisputed, such as the emergence of cybercrime as a growing phenomenon (see Hoar, 2005; McGuire & Dowling, 2013) not always sufficiently reflected in police statistics (Caneppele & Aebi, 2019; Kemp et al., 2020), others such as the transfer of opportunities from physical space to cyberspace and its impact on crime, especially among the youngest, had barely been noticed (Aebi & Linde, 2010, 2014; Miró-Llinares & Moneva, 2019) and had not yet been sufficiently developed as a plausible conjecture.

The Role of Technology, Opportunity, and Lifestyles Changes on Crime Trends

We should not be surprised that some social and technological changes indirectly cause unexpected shifts in trends. The work that most clearly highlighted the need to reassess the relationship between technological changes and crime trends through the lens of opportunity was conducted by Cohen and Felson in 1979. In their seminal article, Cohen and Felson linked technological developments such as the emergence and popularization of cars and ATMs with changes in lifestyles, creating new convergence opportunities between assailants and victims in the absence of capable guardians.

These ideas have been applied by many authors to explain crime trends, but one of the works that most clearly reflects this relationship, and in particular the impact of the indirect consequences of some technological changes on crime and its trends, is Martin Killias's work (2006) and his Crime Breaches theory. Based on the RAT foundations, Killias points out that increases in crime are often caused by new opportunities that arise for criminals due to technological or social changes, lasting until a defensive response is produced against them. Examples of "breaches" opened as a result of a socio-technological change would include the expansion of the banking system, the development of air traffic, or the increase in electronic payment systems, which open new opportunities that may take time to respond to. Of course, the emergence of some technologies can be directly related to criminal changes: new weapons, new police tools, etc. However, sometimes, as Cohen and Felson pointed out, technologies are developed or social changes occur that are not directly related to a change in criminal behavior but have "indirect consequences" in changing the way opportunities are generated, either because they increase or decrease them due to the functioning of other essential elements of the criminal event such as the activity of the victims or the surveillance of guardians, place managers, etc.

Another hypothesis, derived from the relationship between criminal opportunity, social and technological change, and crime trends, applied to the so-called crime drop, is the "security hypothesis" (Farrell et al., 2011). Based on the RAT foundations and considering the increase in security investment in most countries in the 1990s, it links changes in the quantity and quality of security with "crime falls in most industrial societies." Although the data used for such claims essentially referred to technological changes related to vehicle theft, the authors have tried to first extend the scope of the theory to other forms of crime related to the hypothesis such as theft (Thompson, 2014) and burglary (Tilley et al., 2015b; Tseloni et al., 2017), and then to make it the main hypothesis for crime drops in general, either under the argument that by preventing these crimes from occurring due to the impact of increased security, potential criminal careers that started with them would have disappeared (the debut crime hypothesis; Farrell et al., 2011), or by constituting vehicle theft as a keystone crime facilitating other crimes. Here, the theory struggles more in the attempt to directly relate technological changes associated with increased security in homes and vehicles to the decline in other forms of crime, particularly violent crime (Ganpat et al., 2020). In fact, the main weakness of the security hypothesis, in an attitude perhaps too similar to that of Isaiah Berlin's hedgehog in "using one idea for everything," is the attempt to explain all or the main crime drops since the 1990s based on a single change. The improvement of some security technologies might have had an impact, whether or not concurrent with other factors, on some specific forms of crime (Farrell et al., 2011), but it is unlikely to fully explain all the concurrent trends, deviations, and nuances that fall within what has been termed the crime drop (Farrall, 2017). Perhaps the promising nature of the hypothesis and the solidity of its empirical foundation in relation to some specific types of crime have made us forget how difficult it is for such a significant, global, and diverse trend in crime types, offenders, and victims to have such a specific and unique origin. Therefore, it is advisable to broaden our view beyond the increase in security to the changes in opportunities that a broader and more complex process might be producing.

The security hypothesis had been proposed by Killias and Aebi (2000) and Aebi (2004) to explain crime trends in Europe almost a decade before Farrell et al. (2011) started insisting on its pertinence to explain the crime drop. Similarly, Aebi and Linde's insistence on the role of the internet on lifestyles and consequently on crime trends has been almost systematically ignored by other researchers working on that topic (Aebi & Linde, 2010, 2012a, b, 2014). Perhaps their mistake was to take for granted that the role of internet was so important that it did not need a deep development. It is only 10 years after their first article that they insisted specifically on it. Hence, Linde and Aebi (2020) provided evidence that digitalization was a change even larger than modernization because it affected the whole world and not only the Western countries that would become known as developed. They also show that digitalization implies a paradigm shift and they trace their origins to those of computerization in the 1950s, the arrival of video games in the 1970s and 1980s, internet in 1992, and the smartphones in 2007 (Linde & Aebi, 2020).

Until then, Aebi and Linde had written about the period before the arrival of smartphones and paid special attention to the access to the internet. Hence, in 2010 and in the framework of their multifactor explanation of crime trends in Western Europe, they stated that the rapid expansion of the internet began in the 1990s and significantly influenced lifestyles, particularly among young people. This shift resulted in youths spending more time at home engaged in virtual activities and less time in public spaces, thereby reducing their likelihood of participating in activities that could lead to crime (Agnew, 2009). However, Aebi and Linde (2010) pointed out that access to the internet was unevenly distributed, largely dependent on the socioeconomic status of families. Youths from medium or high socioeconomic backgrounds spend less time in public places and are less likely to commit conventional crimes but more likely to engage in computer-related offenses, such as hacking or credit card fraud. These types of crimes have only recently been tracked by European police statistics, making historical data limited (Aebi et al., 2010; Jehle & Harrendorf, 2010). Conversely, youths from lower socioeconomic backgrounds, including many from ethnic minorities, are more likely to spend time in public spaces, increasing their risk of involvement in street gangs or unsupervised activities that can lead to crime (Aebi & Linde, 2010).

Later, Aebi and Linde (2014) extended their explanation in an article that examines homicide trends in 15 West European countries from 1960 to 2010, revealing a linear increase in homicide victimization from the mid-1960s to the early 1990s, followed by a linear decrease until 2010. Aebi and Linde (2014) propose a lifestyle approach to explain these trends. The 1960s marked a significant turning point, characterized by a relaxation of social norms, increased leisure activities, and the emergence of youth subcultures such as rock and roll and street gangs. Key lifestyle changes during this period included greater social freedom, the availability of contraceptives, and the integration of women into the labor market, all of which contributed to shifts in crime victimization patterns including a rise of homicides that coincides with the predictions of Cohen and Felson (1979). In the 1990s, another major lifestyle shift occurred, driven largely by the reunification of Europe and the rise of the internet. The internet revolutionized how young people spent their leisure time, resulting in more time spent at home and less time in public spaces. This shift reduced opportunities for conventional crimes but increased opportunities for computer-related offenses (Aebi & Linde, 2014).

Indeed, the early developments of RAT (Cohen & Felson, 1979) somehow blended the spirit of the fox and the hedgehog, looking at multiple social changes but linking them all behind a single mechanism of opportunity convergence. Various social and technological changes would have converged in an increase in crime, contradicting the explanatory hypotheses of traditional criminology. Specifically, these varied unexpected changes in lifestyles, in turn derived from the emergence of technologies, would, through the mechanism of necessary convergence between motivated assailants, suitable victims, and in the absence of guardians and managers, explain many of the increases or decreases in crime. Just as Cohen and Felson observed that there were large and diverse social changes that had occurred in the 1960s (the emergence of the automobile or the labor insertion of women), a thorough analysis of the reasons for the decline in crime since the 1990s requires to review other social changes that could alter criminal opportunities in the sense of reducing them. And while it is true that from the 1990s technology increased security in cars and homes, the great technological revolution that began to manifest itself from that decade worldwide, and which could have had more effects than imagined, was the digitalization process. This revolution not only facilitated other security technologies but also changed the way people relate to each other, their social habits, and thus could have altered some criminal opportunities.

Building on these theoretical bases and with the aforementioned scientific attitude, the present work develops a conjecture that may seem strange to those unfamiliar but is behind, like an elephant in the room, many of the ideas about recent crime trends: What if what links both the slow declining trend in crime since the 90s and the abrupt decline during the Covid-19 pandemic lockdowns is the change in opportunities produced by changes in mobility habits from the streets to homes, caused since the 90s by the digitalization process (among other factors) and abruptly accelerated for a short period of time due to the confinement during the pandemic? According to this, both declining crime trends, slow in one case and abrupt in the other, reflect social changes that are directly or indirectly related to technological changes in individual and social habits and the indirect appearance or reduction of criminal opportunities. The reduction of mobility in urban areas and in relation to some activities during the Covid-19 pandemic (see Felson et al., 2020; Hodgkinson & Andresen, 2020; Ashby, 2020) would have resulted in a decrease in street crime due to the decrease in opportunities there (Halford et al., 2020; Shen et al., 2021; Abrams, 2020), while digitalization would have allowed new opportunities in homes due to increased time spent there and increased internet use. Something similar, but at a much slower and less perceptible pace, could have occurred in relation to the advent of digital technology in our societies since the mid-1990s and the following decade. The emergence of digitalization in its various stages would have reduced, especially among young people who more rapidly adopted these technologies, some activities that were carried out in physical space and that now, when carried out at home, first with video games and then on the internet, reduced criminal opportunities in physical space.

The Disputed, But Always Alive, Hypothesis of a Relationship Between Digitalization and the Offline Crime Drop (and Its Misunderstandings)

An Overview of Studies on the Link Between Digitalization and the Offline Crime Drop

When analyzing the foundations upon which literature has built this potential relationship between digitalization and crime in each of the two most recent trends that have sparked academic interest, it is advisable to begin with two interconnected considerations. The first is that this supposed relationship between digital development, particularly the advent of the internet, and the decline in crime known as The Great American Crime Decline or "The Crime Drop," is somewhat counterintuitive. One would expect the emergence of this new technology to result in new goods to steal and new ways of committing crimes, which should have led to an increase in property crimes initially, followed by numerous other forms of criminality as social networks and other forms of personal contact became possible through the internet. In fact, some authors point out that this is what could have happened in relation to general crime rates, and if it is not observed in official figures, it is due to the enormous amount of unreported crimes, higher than in other forms of criminality (Graham et al., 2019). As argued later, some of these two ideas are compatible with each other, and a thorough examination of how digitalization occurred and the effects of each of its development stages will show us how social life communicates and what happens in one sphere can affect another distinct one. However, to begin with, and since data on an ongoing social revolution always take time to appear, it seems reasonable that literature would scarcely resort to this idea to explain the crime drop. This is the second consideration: The conjecture that will be defended here, linking some of the declines in crime framed in the crime drop to changes in the leisure habits of certain population groups toward spending more time at home and less on the street, originated from the digital revolution that began to manifest itself in those years, has never been a favorite hypothesis of authors to explain the crime drop. Perhaps, as Green has pointed out, this oversight can be explained by the gradual and imperceptible way in which these technologies have enveloped us and made their way into all aspects of our daily lives, "reconstituting our social fabric" (Green, 2016).

However, it must also be acknowledged that this idea has always fluttered as one of the possible causes of some of the drops, especially by authors who base their explanatory starting point on the routine activity theory (RAT). In fact, it is striking, given the contrast with the later understanding of the scarce plausibility of the relationship between the digital revolution and the crime drop (Farrell & Birks, 2018, 2020), but somewhat logical given its entanglement with RAT theory, that from the very appearance of the so-called security hypothesis, the idea of the role that the internet could be playing in crime trends was already present in the works of Tilley, Farrell, or Tseloni. Firstly, when they pointed out that most theories did not explain the increase in crimes committed through the internet (Farrell et al., 2014), although they did not develop the argument much further, and secondly, when Tilley and Farrell themselves, joined by Clarke for that work, explicitly recognized that the decline in crime due to the reduction of opportunities could originate from, alongside the already defended "intended improvements in security" and the "unintended improvements in security," the "unintended effects of routine activities (changed lifestyles, socioeconomic, political, and technological progress)" (Tilley et al., 2015a), although they also did not develop this idea at all, and a specific author later considered it a coincidence (Farrell & Birks, 2018) due to the supposed lack of data to support it, as will be discussed in more detail later (Farrell & Birks, 2020). It could be argued, using Paul Knepper's apt comment, that any good theory on history has to assume the lack of data and not dismiss a hypothesis for not having them (Knepper, 2018).

Nevertheless, what truly merits emphasis at this juncture is that, barring a few specific exceptions, for those who believe that opportunity plays a significant role in the macroevolution of crime because it does so at the micro-level, the digital revolution, internet, and their coinciding with the crime drop have always been present as, at the very least, a plausible idea worth exploring. This seems logical when considering the intriguing parallel between two opposing trends: the increase in crime during the 60s and 70s, which laid the groundwork for the routine activity theory (RAT) approach, and the decrease in criminal activity in the 90s, which immediately renders this a promising hypothesis directly derived from the broader framework of RAT and opportunity. In the article by Cohen and Felson, the shift from a previous downward trend in crime to an upward one in the 70s was explained by an increase in the convergence opportunities between aggressors and victims caused by social and technological changes. Conversely, the opposing shift that likely began in the 90s could be attributed to different types of social and technological changes that would have resulted in the inverse effect: a decrease in convergence opportunities stemming from changes in lifestyles. If the technological changes of the 70s, such as the popularization of automobiles and increased mobility, or the proliferation of ATMs and the availability of cash, generated more opportunities and, with them, an unexpected increase in crime, then the factors that would have decreased them in the 90s would include, among others, technological changes that led to reduced mobility and opportunities on the streets, as well as increased time spent at home. In the 90s, and then continuing into the 2000s maintaining the downward trend, what began to change people's lives, and particularly to increase the time young people spent at home, was computing, video games, and all forms of digital leisure.

Broadly speaking, this was the starting point for the initial authors who explicitly proposed this explanatory hypothesis, specifying its relevance to young people and the types of crime more directly associated with them. Clearly, in 2010, Aebi and Linde sought to find an explanation for the increase in violent crimes in Europe. Starting from the usual overrepresentation of minors as perpetrators of such offenses (Farrington, 2003; Sampson & Laub, 2003), they focused on changes in the lifestyle of young people, particularly those due to the massive development of the internet since the 90s. They identified a lifestyle change in terms of free time usage, characterized by spending significantly more time at home in front of their computers, connected to virtual social networks, online games, and a variety of electronic communication tools. This, in turn, results in less time spent on the streets and in public places, reducing the chances of finding oneself in situations leading to delinquency (Agnew, 2009: 183). Although the hypothesis also included a reference to the parallel increase in opportunities to participate in new crimes arising with the development of cyberspace, this, however, as later confirmed, would not be reflected in official statistics due to the dark figure problem of cybercrime (Caneppele & Aebi, 2019). The central point of the argument, clearly influenced by RAT, consisted of linking the advent of the internet with young people spending more time at home, and this lifestyle change with the decline in crime, drawing heavily on the evolution of internet use in Europe during the period under consideration. Later, they extended this line of thinking to the study of homicide trends from 1950 to 2010 linking RAT and lifestyle theory (Hindelang et al., 1978).

Subsequently, in a theoretical paper, Green (2016) was surprised that most scholars studying the crime drop continued to overlook the importance of the spectacular expansion of the media landscape since the 1980s. He developed a hypothesis on the impact of changes in media consumption on the decline in street crime based on three mechanisms: (a) the displacement of an unknown but significant number of street crimes to crimes committed online; (b) the alteration of lifestyle patterns in terms of spending more time at home, especially by young people (those most prone to crime), resulting in a decrease in opportunities to commit it; and (c) because the rise of social media and networks would have facilitated the development of extensive social networks among young people, reducing their propensity to commit crimes in various ways consistent with established criminological theory. However, this work was theoretical and highlighted the notorious difficulty of isolating and empirically demonstrating such a hypothesis, using Knepper's words to argue that "the influence of the Internet on the crime drop is 'incalculable'" (Knepper, 2018, p. 71). There is merit to both points, but it is striking that no empirical studies supporting very similar hypotheses were taken into account to strengthen these interesting propositions, especially in relation to delinquent opportunities and changes in minors' leisure habits and increased time spent at home due to changes in leisure habits among minors.

We specifically refer to the nearly forgotten but extremely interesting work of Jeremy Don Kerr, in which, utilizing the routine activity theory (RAT) approach, he strives to understand the changes in crime rates from 1978 to 2002 (Kerr, 2005). Kerr starts from an initial observation: the apparent contradiction between Cohen and Felson's hypothesis that living in a single-person household or the incorporation of women into the workforce exposed individuals to a higher risk of property victimization at home, and to a higher risk of violent victimization for women, compared with the lower levels of property victimization in single-person households and the reduction in female victimization in 2002 to one-third of the 1978 levels. From this point, Kerr looks for structural and technological changes that would have caused an increase in the amount of time spent at home, thus explaining the reduction in opportunities for crime, and focuses on the "technological transformation of leisure," which, although originating with the emergence of radio, film, and television, intensified in the 80s and 90s with digitalization, the advent of cable television, video games, and computers, all contributing to transforming the use of free time. Kerr's hypothesis, therefore, is as anticipated: Technological changes between 1978 and 2002 increased the amount of leisure time people spend in domestic contexts where the convergence of motivated offenders, suitable targets, and the lack of a capable guardian is relatively unlikely, thus contributing to the decline in victimization rates. To confirm this, he analyzes victimization data from the NCVS for the period 1978–2002 for robbery, theft, and violent victimization of different groups of people and compares them with six variables related to technological leisure activities: (1) the percentage of households with cable, (2) the percentage of households with VHR, (3) the percentage of households with personal computers, (4) the percentage of households with internet access, (5) the average number of units of video rental and sale, and (6) the average household sales of video game hardware and software. The tech-leisure index was strongly and significantly associated with the rate of theft and burglary, even when controlling for other factors. The tech-leisure index was also associated with violent crimes, though less strongly than for property crimes, and the relationship was statistically significant for white victimization, male victimization, female victimization, victimization of individuals aged 12 to 34, as well as for individuals aged 35 and over. The relationship between the tech-leisure index and black victimization was relatively weak, and the relationship was not statistically significant (Kerr, 2005).

Kerr's analyses, therefore, support the hypothesis that the technological transformation of leisure is partly responsible for the changes in crime victimization rates that began in the 80s and became more significant from the mid-90s onward (Kerr, 2005). And the argument is no longer just that young people are less involved in criminal activities by spending more time at home but that the increase in the amount of leisure time people spend at home has also increased surveillance against property crimes at home and helped to reduce the exposure of potential victims to motivated offenders in contexts that lack adequate surveillance, thus reducing the rates of violent victimization. Furthermore, Kerr's study offers interesting nuances, such as the weak association of the tech-leisure index with female violent victimization consistent both with their greater victimization within the home and with the fact that some activities, such as video games, are more linked to men; or the lack of correlation with victimization in black men, explainable by the lower penetration of cable television, computers, and the internet in black households compared to white households (Kerr, 2005). It is true that this study does not allow to determine to what extent the increase in tech-leisure activities represents a real increase in the amount of time or in the proportion of time that people spend at home, since the increase in tech-leisure activities could also be reflecting a redistribution of leisure activities within the home. However, other research has begun to fill such gaps.

Consequently, some research endeavors examining the relationship between video games and crime from a macro perspective prove to be particularly intriguing. Contrary to the socially accepted hypothesis that video games might generate violence and increase crime rates, these studies have found a negative correlation between the increased time spent playing video games at home and crime. This was initially discovered by Ward, who started from the hypothesis that video games would be associated with a higher prevalence of violent criminal behavior (murders, rapes, robberies, assaults, etc.) (Ward, 2011). To test this, they used a data panel from 400 states in the United States, spanning from 1994 to 2004, to compare the number of video game stores to the number of crimes committed. The results were entirely contrary to predictions, showing that the number of video game stores was associated with significant decreases in crime rates. This conclusion challenges the historic hypothesis that playing violent video games would lead to aggressive behaviors, supposedly culminating in an increase in violent crime in cities where video games had become popular. This relationship between violent video games and a decrease in crime is clear for property crimes but less evident for violent crimes. Following this line of inquiry, McCaffree and Proctor (2017) analyzed, through the construction of a composite data panel (crimes known to the police in each state, video game behavior rates, estimated consumer spending rates, state census, etc.), the hypothesis for 50 US states for the years 1997, 2001, and 2003. They postulated that as long as video games are played at home, this should correlate negatively with the commission of violent and property crimes. The results confirmed this hypothesis, finding a negative relationship between the percentage of individuals playing video games at home and property crimes, such as theft or vehicle robbery.

In the case of violent crimes, a study by Breuer et al. analyzed the relationship between aggression and violent games in a sample of 276 players aged between 14 and 21 years through a longitudinal study spanning 1 year (Breuer et al., 2015). This study concluded that the use of violent video games in young Germans is not a substantial predictor of physical aggression. Similarly, Ferguson's research on juvenile violence and the consumption of violent video games between 1966 and 2011 suggests the existence of an inverse relationship, although a causal relationship cannot be determined (Ferguson, 2015). A recent study on the popular and highly violent game Grand Theft Auto V conducted a time-series analysis of the number of crimes recorded in the Dutch Offender Index for males aged 12–25 and the daily number of GTAV players from its release to 2 years later (Beerthuizen et al., 2017). The results showed a statistically significant negative association between the number of crimes and GTAV players. Lastly, in 2021, Baumer, Cundiff, and Luo analyzed the change in the prevalence of juvenile delinquency in America, concluding that the increase in computers, the internet, and video games within homes had produced a new form of digital socialization among young people. This, in turn, has contributed to a reduction in crime rates.

These studies, analyzing the impact on crime at the micro-level of this shift in digital leisure for minors, reinforce the hypothesis, recently defended in an article, that some of the "drops," specifically in juvenile delinquency in the mid-90s, are related to digitalization (Miró-Llinares & Moneva, 2019). An indirect effect of digitalization, such as the increased time young people spend at home, could be related to the decrease in arrests for vandalism and other forms of delinquency associated with young people in the United States that began in the mid-90s, as derived from that research, a trend that also occurred in a similar manner in England and Wales (Miró-Llinares & Moneva, 2019). And then came the internet. Since the late 90s, when the use of the internet began to become popular, there has been an increase in the number of households with internet access, the use of digital platforms, and also the use of video games among young people (The Nielsen Company, 2018). This change in IT usage trends for leisure, particularly for young people, would explain—at least partially—the increased time spent at home, resulting in a subsequent reduction of opportunities in the physical space and an increase in opportunities in cyberspace. This topic will be discussed later.

However, it is crucial not to fall into the Hedgehog's mindset and think that everything is exclusively due to a single social change, namely, the change in leisure habits at home and the reduction of time young people spend on the streets. A technological revolution as significant as digitalization requires to continue broadening our focus in line with Cohen and Felson's work, paying attention to other changes that may have affected opportunity and that are directly or indirectly related to technology. Academia has identified other potential changes related to the advent of digital technology that may have contributed to a reduction in some crime opportunities related to property crime. A paradigmatic case is the progressive substitution of cash for other payment methods and its direct impact on reducing property crime and an indirect impact on other forms of crime in the United States. According to Wright et al. (2017), this relationship with cash is because, to a large extent, street crime is motivated by a need for cash, as in many cases it is used for activities in which other forms of payment are not accepted. In their research on crime trends in Missouri between 1990 and 2011, they found that the implementation of the Electronic Benefit Transfer (EBT) program to issue food stamps to beneficiaries electronically instead of via checks not only reduced the amount of cash but also resulted in reductions in total crime (16%), robbery offenses (13%), theft offenses (16.3%), and assaults (22.7%), without any noticeable changes in other forms of crime like rape, which are not associated with the presence of cash. Later, Hunt confirmed the same hypothesis at the national level, finding similar patterns in crime reduction. Specifically, the implementation of the EBT was responsible for a 1.3% reduction in street crime nationwide. Hunt concludes that the reduction of cash could explain part of the crime drop in the United States but could also imply a displacement of crime to digital environments, as "the type of crime that occurs is related to the form of currency used" (Hunt, 2017 p. 73). Similarly, Pridemore et al. (2018) conducted a transnational study on the relationship between crime and the payment of social assistance funds, finding that the lack of cash payments was significantly and negatively associated with robbery rates in different countries, with no relationship found with burglaries or homicides.

Beyond Misunderstandings: On the "Heart," Chronology, and Scope of the Conjecture

While some authors, ourselves included, have proposed that certain declines in property and urban crime perpetrated by youth could be attributed to changes in their habits, such as increased time spent at home due to video games and the shift to digital leisure, or the gradual replacement of cash, it is noteworthy that not only do the majority of authors attempting to identify the causes of the "crime drops" not attribute a central role to this factor, but there are also those who, despite seemingly holding compatible views on the significance of opportunity, exhibit considerable resistance to acknowledging the relevance of this relationship between the advent of digital technology and the crime drop, perceiving the concurrent trends as little more than a coincidence (Farrell & Birks, 2018, 2020).

We suggest that this is due to misunderstandings surrounding the meaning and scope of this conjecture, which hadn't been fully developed and should be elaborated on in more detail. Having achieved a more detailed description, a clarification of these misunderstandings is aimed at developing more specific hypotheses and testing them. In concrete, three misunderstandings of the relationship between digital technologies and crime drops are identified.

The first misunderstanding concerns the connection between crime drop and the rise of cybercrime. The second one has to do with the lack of synchrony between the beginning of the crime drop and the appearance of cybercrime and the internet. As a derivative of the first argument, this misunderstanding is a result of the misidentification of the core of the relationship between digitalization and opportunity. The third misunderstanding concerns the scope of the hypothesis which deserves further nuancing. Each of these issues will be briefly developed in the following paragraphs.

Starting with the relationship between cybercrime and crime drops, it is widely recognized that parallel to the decline of some forms of crime, especially property-based crime in the "meat space" (Pease, 2003), the development of information technology (IT) began to exhibit new opportunities for crime, with IT being either a tool for or an object of attack. Despite the difficulties surrounding the proper definition, detection, and measurement of cybercrime through official statistics (Wall, 2007) and their incapacity to reflect its very high number of unrecorded cases, the emergence of new crime types connected to IT (i.e., cyber-dependent crimes) could be observed as well as criminal behaviors that replicate existing crimes such as fraud, harassment, etc., in cyberspace (i.e., cyber-enabled crimes). From its occasional appearance in the 70s and 80s, including the first and most relevant types of computer crime in the 1990s (see Parker & Nycum, 1984; Parker, 1989; Easttom et al., 2011), a new trend arose which would significantly increase with the development of the internet throughout the 2000s. In short, the increase of crime in cyberspace paralleled the decline of crime in the physical space.

This concurrence of opposite trends over time has been analyzed with different purposes and in different ways: Some used the increase in "internet-related crimes" to question the consistency of some theories of the crime drop (Farrell et al., 2011) but without explaining the reason or drawing any consequence for their hypotheses from the appearance of online crimes (which they identified in the early 90s). Other authors have used the trend to second-guess the crime drop itself, highlighting that with the total sum of infractions, it might have been wrong to speak of a decrease in property crime since the observed decrease would only apply to physical space. This is the case of Canneppele and Aebi (2019) who point at the evolution of cybercrime as a missing element considering that the rise of online and hybrid crimes has contributed to the drop of online crimes after confirming the insufficiency of official statistics to include cybercrimes and considering what is being left out to explain the crime drop. This does not mean that the authors explain one trend via the other since they expressly point out that this does not imply that the rise of cybercrime was the cause of the drop of traditional crime recalling the temporal inconsistency between the emergence of both trends pointed out by Farrell et al. (2014). They do, however, consider that the increase in cybercrime has contributed to intensifying the decline in traditional crime against property since the year 2000. However, how is this seemingly causal relationship to be specified? Are they specifically referring to a direct link between the micro mechanism of both trends, in the sense that criminals abandon crimes in the physical space in favor of new criminal opportunities in cyberspace? Would this mechanism explain the global trend from 2000 onward and extend into the present? It is obvious that the authors are not defending the idea of a direct connection between both tendencies. They are defending an indirect connection through the mechanism of opportunity. This mechanism links the decrease of opportunities in physical space to digitalization, in the sense that young adults spend more time at home, and thus aren't confronted with the opportunity of crime in the physical space. In turn, the appearance of new criminal opportunities related to the use of the internet and digital devices and its popularization at a universal level confront them with new criminal opportunities.

We acknowledge that data is still far too sparse to identify the exact causal mechanism by which this occurs. Reference to the fact that cybercrime contributed to the decrease in physical property crime after the 2000s does, however, permit a more detailed exploration of this relationship. Other authors, who linked the decrease of offline property crime with its increase online (e.g., Tcherni et al., 2015; Button & Cross, 2017; Williams & Levi, 2017), are contradicted by Farrell and Birks (2018), who maintain a lack of solid evidence to support the hypothesis that cybercrime caused the crime drop. They furthermore argue the temporal inconsistency between both trends and especially the lack of a causal mechanism that explains the transfer from physical crime to cybercrime. Even though the nature of Farrell and Birks's argument has been shown, which refutes the relationship between changes in lifestyles produced by the internet and crime trends (Miró-Llinares & Moneva, 2019), interests lies in briefly reflecting on the reasons that Farrell and Birks state in their rejection of the relationship between the increase in cybercrime and some of the effects of the crime drop.

Firstly, Farrell and Birks's "causal mechanism" argument consists in refuting the plausibility of an idea that hadn't been explicitly supported in the literature, namely, that "the primary mechanism by which cybercrime is assumed to induce the crime drop is attractive displacement: offenders substituting more attractive online crime for their physical crime" (Farrell & Birks, 2018, p. 2). The authors state that it is difficult to imagine that cybercrime could replace street robberies, given the different skills they require, and that someone would stop stealing in the street to commit cybercrimes. To show the incoherence of the argument, they recur to the example of the increase in mobile phone thefts in the 1990s. While it is true that some cybercrimes require a set of skills that traditional criminals don't, some less technical types of cybercrime may be covered by individuals and criminal organizations (Miró & Johnson, 2017). The main error in the argument, however, lies in construing the connection between the opposing trends as a direct shift of individual perpetrators from one type of delinquency to the other. Cohen and Felson (1979) showed that one has to look not only at expected effects but also at the unexpected, meaning that a third, unknown element may be directly related to both trends and govern their relationship. As has been already stated elsewhere (Miró-Llinares & Moneva,

2019), the process of social digitalization that began to manifest itself in the 90s and gained strength throughout the 2000s had causal effects on the reduction of opportunities in the physical space by the greater time spent at home due to the rise of digital leisure for young people who are more likely to commit crimes if they are on the streets, and in the increase in criminal opportunity for all those who were beginning to be in the cyberspace. A plausible alternative explanation for the convergence of these trends is not the one Farrell and Birks argue against, nor does it rely on "mere chance," because it relays these tendencies indirectly. There is no need for a car thief to become a hacker to explain the decrease in car thefts in terms of the increase in cybercrime. As long as young people reduce the time spent on the street and therefore are less involved in criminal activities and, simultaneously, other young people in the houses discover and become involved in other illicit opportunities, this explanation holds on a macro-level. It is only correct to say that they are independent trends (Farrell & Birks, 2018) if the core of the causal relationship is misidentified. As mentioned before, it is the opportunity, in this case, provided by the digitalization process, that creates a connection between two apparently independent trends. Thus, if the crime drop is related to general trends of digitalization and the specific lifestyle changes this brings about rather than to cybercrime in particular, the connection becomes apparent: Cybercrime does not mutate or reduce criminal opportunity by increasing leisure and other activities at home (and reducing, that way, unstructured socializing), but digitalization does, especially since the appearance of the internet.

Admittedly, it could still be argued that the "causal mechanism" linking the change in habits brought about by digitalization, specifically in the form of increased time at home, to reduced crime is still missing. It has already been pointed out that less time on the streets means, per se, a reduction in opportunities for crime. But then, in addition, there is a direct way of linking less time on the streets with juvenile delinquency. Before going into this, however, another misunderstanding needs to be resolved.

The accurate identification of the core of the hypothesis also serves to redress this second criticism that results from the first misunderstanding, namely, that of temporal inconsistency (Farrell & Birks, 2018). When the possible connection between the crime drop and cybercrime/internet/cyberspace is brought up, so is the idea that while the decline in property crime usually dates back to the early 1990s (and even earlier in the United States for certain crimes), at that time, the internet had barely been established in most of the world. This inconsistency in timing lets Farrell and Birks (2018) consider the temporal correlation in cases like Australia, where crime against property began to decrease in 2001 (Farrell & Birks, 2018) "more adulterated than causal." They base their claim on the requirement included in "the varying trajectories test" which states that any hypothesis must be capable of explaining the differences between the periods in the trends of the different crime types and in different countries. Farrell rightly points out (2013) that a theoretical hypothesis that attempts to explain the crime drop must be flexible enough to take all temporal variations between countries into account. This criterion is not fulfilled in the case of the "cybercrime hypothesis." According to Farrell and Birks, cybercrime came too late and spread too slowly to cause crime to drop; moreover, it's not plausible to the authors that its increase in the twenty-first century had a causal effect on crime "since adolescent offending rates were already decimated and there was no acceleration in the rate of decline in physical crimes" (p. 2).

As these considerations show, the critical argument of "temporary inconsistency" is not only directed against the hypothesis of cybercrime but, implicitly, against the impact of the internet, the changes in lifestyles it provokes, and the resulting impact on crime drops, such as the timing of the crime drop in the United States, taking into account recent discoveries regarding differences across age cohorts. The focus is placed on two aspects: on the one hand, on his understanding that the starting point of any hypothesis on the impact of digitalization must start from the 2000s and the impacts of the popularization of the internet, and on the other hand, on the underlying claim that there cannot be causes that concur in the explanation of a trend that can add their effects in different moments in time, among others.

Regarding the first, the problem lies in a misidentification of the core of the hypothesis and the essential causal mechanism that explains the connection among the analyzed trends: If the central element of the hypothesis is cybercrime as a new criminal phenomenon (Miró-Llinares, 2012), with the appearance of both new attractive suitable targets in cyberspace and potentially more profitable criminal activities on the internet as critical elements of the argument, the identification of the beginning twenty-first century as a starting point for the crime drop is a viable conclusion. Since it wasn't until the 2000s that cybercrime was a widespread reality, the 90s should have been relatively unaffected by the crime drop. Even though the first attacks on computer systems utilizing destructive viruses, that is the first computer crimes, were executed in the 70s and 80s (Parker, 1989; Easttom et al., 2011), and cybercrime became more prevalent in the 90s, it wasn't until the popularization of the internet, beginning the 2000s, and even more so with the appearance of the web 2.0 and smartphones since 2005, that cybercrime increased massively. However, as mentioned before, there is another way to relate both trends, focusing on the habits and opportunities that changed because of digitalization rather than cybercrime and the internet. Digitalization had already arrived in the 80s and proliferated especially in the mid to late 90s and was already affecting, along with other changes in leisure, the time that young people spent at home and, subsequently the crime opportunities that this entailed (Green, 2016). This point will be examined further below in greater depth. It is, furthermore, possible that digitalization first produced effects in the reduction of opportunities in the physical space due to the aforementioned behavioral changes (e.g., the personal computer and video games) and that increases in the opportunities in cyberspace wouldn't come about until later, due to a different mechanism such as the appearance of the internet and the possibility of committing crimes remotely.

This is related to the second clarification of the critical argument of temporal asynchrony and the scope of the general hypothesis of the existence of a relationship between the digitalization process and the crime drop. The fact that a decrease in delinquency and an increase in time spent at home are unsynchronized in the beginning doesn't contradict the possibility of a common origin, even though they may not converge until later (Miró-Llinares & Moneva, 2019). In point and fact, the consideration that cybercrime can't have caused the crime drop because the development of the internet and cybercrime came later rests upon the idea that there must have been a unique and original cause that not only triggered the effect of a decrease in delinquency but also kept it permanent over time. Even though this may in principle be the case, it is not a parsimonious presumption to think that all criminal typologies that suffered a decrease did so due to the same cause, and to further believe that this cause was maintained over a long period of time, producing continuous effects of crime decrease, means to introduce additional assumptions. It seems more reasonable to accept that there were several decreases and that they may, at least in part, be caused by different factors. In the same way, it is reasonable to assume that the initial decline was caused by one factor but that other factors favored the continuation of this trend. And this must also be related to the weight that different cohorts at different times may have had on the overall decline in crime. As other research has shown, the mechanism that would drive down crime rates in general need not be an effect that acts on all members of society equally and always in the same way. In the case of crime drop, some consider it more reasonable to think of it as a cohort effect, an age-period interaction or a cohort-period interaction (Kim et al., 2016; Matthews & Minton, 2018), or that there is a sum of particular factors affecting the fall in crime rates at different periods (Humphreys et al., 2014).

To distance ourselves from monocausal cum *hoc ergo propter hoc* theories, that explore singular potential causes for tendencies that lasted for over 25 years (e.g., the security hypothesis; Farrell et al., 2011), more specific effects of the impact of digitalization on crime drops have to be explored. Only then it is possible to move away from arguments that default to the best temporally suiting societal phenomenon as the driver of the crime drop. Tendencies are not monolithic and have to be explained as a compound of smaller effects, especially phenomena as dissimilar and diverse as those that add up to "patrimonial and violent crime in Western societies." "Digitalization" and "crime drop" are, rather than "things," macro reflections of plural, diverse, and generally multicausal events that evolve and change over time. In other words, and for the purpose of this chapter, it is possible that cybercrime, the internet, and digitalization as well as their effects on opportunities did not coincide with the beginning of the descending trend in crime. It is therefore reasonable to say that they were not "the" cause of the decline in the early years. But not only has it been observed, and will be explored in greater depth, that some of the elements of digitalization had already begun to change lifestyles but also that it is possible that the downward trends in criminal tendencies were stabilized by new, unexpected, causes.

The explicit or implicit rejection of the idea that co-occurring causes aggregate their effects on a given trend at different times is not reasonable. Of course, the necessity to explore the connection between processes of digitalization that were experienced since the 1990s and the crime trends in recent years is defended, and why it is believed that some of the down and upward trends can be explained through this framework. But it is not denied that these may coincide with other processes of concomitant causal incidence. This is particularly the case in regard to what has been called crime drop which, despite having been seen as a monolithic phenomenon, contains various tendencies which did not occur in the same way in all places (Aebi & Linde, 2010), at the same time, for all crimes and all cohorts. From this perspective, and in an analogy to the routine activity theory (RAT) which was first applied to construe changes in crime trends between the 1950s and the 1970s, it is reasonable to posit that several factors have impacted a great variety of criminal typologies and opportunities, leading to the complicated composition of phenomena that are reduced to the terms cybercrime, digitalization, and crime drop.

The Literature on Youth Crime Trends (Beyond the Crime Drop), a New Clue to the Conjecture

The conjecture upheld in this book, which links crime trends—particularly some of the decreases in crime rates of certain forms of crime since the 1990s until mid of the 2010s—has been previously mentioned as not intending to serve as a comprehensive explanation for what came to be termed the offline "crime drop." Rather, it should be seen as one cause among others that explains some of the decreases. Specifically, the conjecture is directly related to the decrease in crime within a particular cohort, namely, that of the youth and young adults. This demographic typically has, for various reasons, a more substantial overall impact on changes in crime rates (Aebi & Linde, 2010, 2014). It can be preliminarily stated, though it will be further discussed later, that the reason for the special relationship between digitalization and youth is that the latter were more significantly affected by technological change and were quicker to alter their habits and routines. However, if this is the case, and given that digitalization has proven to be a slow, staged revolution that has been underway for some time and has become universal (albeit at different paces in different countries), information from observing the trends in crimes committed by minors and young adolescents over recent decades could potentially provide clues about the causal mechanism linking digitalization and the associated changes in youth habits with the reduction in crime.

The most recent literature has demonstrated a trend of decreasing crime perpetrated by minors and young adults, both among males and females, though the decline is greater in the former in some studies (Estrada et al., 2016; Keyes et al., 2018), across various countries and types of offenses. Although there are differences in when the trend began, due in part to the different data sources used for analysis (self-reporting or police-recorded data), existing studies typically place the start in the early or mid-1990s (Andersen et al., 2016; Arnett, 2018; Elonheimo, 2014; Estrada, 2019; Fernández-Molina & Bartolomé Gutiérrez, 2018, Kivivuori & Bernburg, 2011), though some report a later start in the early 2000s (Holanda (van der Laan et al., 2021)). These declines have been described in the United States (Arnett, 2018; Baumer et al., 2018; Grucza et al., 2018; Keyes et al., 2018; Moss et al., 2019), Oceania countries such as Australia (Payne et al., 2018) and New

Zealand (Polglase & Lambie, 2023), and Europe, including central and northern continental countries like the Netherlands (Berghuis & de Waard, 2017; van der Laan et al., 2019), Denmark (Andersen et al., 2016), Sweden (Estrada, 2019; Sivertsson et al., 2019; Svensson & Ring, 2007; Vasiljevic et al., 2020; Svensson & Oberwittler, 2021), Norway (Frøyland, 2022), Finland (Salmi, 2009; Elonheimo, 2014; Kaakinen & Näsi, 2021), and Lithuania (Sakalauskas et al., 2021), as well as in the United Kingdom, in England, Wales, and Scotland (Griffiths & Norris, 2020; Matthews & Minton, 2018), and southern countries such as Spain (Fernández-Molina & Bartolomé Gutiérrez, 2018). Furthermore, the decline has occurred across different types of offenses including vandalism and incivilities, violent crimes, and property crimes, with the latter category showing the most substantial data and, according to some studies, a more pronounced decline (Fernández-Molina & Bartolomé Gutiérrez, 2018; Salmi, 2009; Sivertsson et al., 2019).

As Baumer et al. (2021) have noted, multiple causes have been put forth to explain these simultaneous declines in various countries. Explanations have especially sought deep changes occurring in how young people are raised by their parents (Twenge, 2017), changes in some social norms (Keyes et al., 2012), or the implementation of stricter laws regarding alcohol consumption in urban settings (Carpenter et al., 2007), generally associated with youth delinquency. There has even been an argument linking improvements in gender equality, as part of a shift in the civilizing process, as a potential explanation for such decreases, though how these two outcomes are inferentially related has not been clearly articulated. In terms of opportunity, it has already been pointed out that the so-called "security hypothesis" posits that the increase in control brought about by technological advances in security explains the reduction also among young people (Farrell, 2013), attributing a generally greater involvement of them in certain offenses to explain why the decline has been more significant among the youth (Farrell et al., 2015). Again, this explanation might hold water for some offenses like vehicle theft, but it is less capable of accounting for other forms of crime such as thefts, burglaries, or the decrease in violence itself.

Numerous studies have already suggested that changes in young people's habits might be particularly linked to the reduction of juvenile delinquency (Arnett, 2018; Baumer et al., 2021; Svensson & Oberwittler, 2021). In this vein, Svensson and Oberwittler (2021) propose a plausible interpretation that the decreased time spent outside the home by youth in the 1990s and 2000s, in the company of peers in settings offering limited supervision and abundant opportunities for deviation—including alcohol consumption—is usually associated with engagement in violent actions and property crimes. Arnett (2018) also arrives at this conclusion, presenting evidence of a decreasing trend among American youth in engaging in risky behaviors. The specific case of alcohol consumption, which has shown a significant downward trend among young people during the same period, has also led to substantial literature confirming the trend but debating its causes (Chomynová & Kážmér, 2019; Rossow et al., 2020; Vashishtha et al., 2022). In particular, Rossow et al. (2020) debate whether the internet and ICTs have had a direct relationship with the reduction of alcohol consumption among youth, and while the evolution of the trend and its comparison with the increase in the use of ICTs seems an evident indicator, some studies that have attempted to directly link computer activities among adolescents and alcohol consumption have found no relationship (Vashishtha et al., 2022). It must be recognized that finding direct indicators of a relationship between both factors, as well as measuring it adequately, is complex. It is not so much a matter of whether computers are used or many hours are spent using them but rather whether this entails a change in habits that leads to spending less time outside the home and sharing less time with other young people. In fact, what is not debated in studies on the simultaneous decrease in alcohol consumption in many countries is the explanatory power of the decrease in the frequency of going out with friends. The changes that have occurred in what is called "unorganized socialization with peers," and specifically the reduced time spent going out at night, would have had a significant effect on alcohol consumption among adolescents (Chomynová & Kážmér, 2019; Rossow et al., 2020).

Perhaps the mistake is to try to link digital communication use directly causally with risky behavior, such as alcohol or delinquency, without relating it to an intermediate mechanism of habit change. In this sense, in relation to alcohol, the approaches that recognize multicausality seem the most promising. Thus, Ball et al. (2022) in their study on the decrease in the proportion of alcohol, tobacco, and cannabis use among adolescents in the period 1990–2019 in Australia, England, the Netherlands, New Zealand, and the United States find international evidence that the reduction of unstructured face-to-face time with friends is a common underlying driver to all behaviors. However, they conclude that alongside this situational factor related to the reduction of opportunities to adopt risky behaviors in general, there are also specific factors that have played a significant role in the decrease in tobacco and alcohol use, such as the decrease in approval of these behaviors among adolescents and more restrictive parental norms (Ball et al., 2022). In a subsequent qualitative study exploring changes in the function and social meaning of alcohol consumption (and nonconsumption) by comparing two cohorts separated by about 20 years, they highlight variables that may help explain the decrease in alcohol consumption among youth. These include the decrease in face-to-face social relationships and the emergence of social networks as a central element in the social life of adolescents, which may displace the key functions of drinking and partying, along with other factors such as the greater omnipresence of risk discourses and increased awareness of the health and social risks of alcohol (Ball et al., 2022, 2023).

In relation to delinquency, the work that most clearly points to the explanatory mechanisms of the decrease in juvenile delinquency is that of Baumer et al. (2021). The authors start by recognizing that most of the theories aiming to explain the contemporary decrease in delinquency have been disconnected from the etiological theories of juvenile delinquency, specifically from the need to link the processes of change with increases in the amount of social control to which young people are exposed, decreases in young people's exposure to physical or social environments conducive to delinquency, and/or reductions in the propensities and motivations for criminal behavior among youth (Baumer & Wolff, 2014). And in their study, they find that the factors related to exposure, particularly the decrease in unstructured socialization and alcohol consumption, are most strongly associated with the reduction of juvenile delinquency. The authors suggest that this change may have been driven by the digitalization process, which "has provided young people with unprecedented entertainment options within the home and has allowed them to increasingly develop and foster friendships virtually, resulting in them spending much less time outside the home with their peers in settings that offer limited supervision and abundant opportunities for deviation, including alcohol consumption." This, they argue, makes contemporary youth much less likely to engage in violence and property crimes.

Although the authors prefer not to draw definitive conclusions without further research employing designs suitable for causal inference, the most suggestive aspect of their contribution is how it relates digitalization to a potential causal mechanism of juvenile delinquency: unstructured socialization or time spent with peers. Indeed, routine activity theory postulates that the way in which young people spend their time, the social environments in which they interact, and their behaviors in those social situations can increase the occurrence of criminal behaviors regardless of the general propensity or motivation to commit crimes. In particular, Osgood et al. pointed out that unstructured socialization among youth increases the opportunities and situational pressures for deviation (Osgood et al., 1996; Osgood & Anderson, 2004), and there is substantial empirical support for this relationship with juvenile delinquency (see Hoeben et al., 2016, for a review). Moreover, unstructured socialization is also related to alcohol consumption (Osgood et al., 1996; Hoeben et al., 2016; Meldrum & Leimberg, 2018), a factor that, in turn, is usually related to participation in both violence and property crimes (Felson et al., 2008; Felson & Staff, 2010; Popovici et al., 2012; White et al., 2015). Hence, it is not that the advent of the internet and computers has produced a reduction in alcohol consumption but rather that it has changed habits, increasing the time young people spend at home, reducing unstructured socialization time and, therefore, alcohol consumption, and, through the interaction between both factors, reducing exposure to risky situations for committing violent and property crimes and participation in them. This alteration in the order in which potential inferences between factors are explained brings the positions of Baumer and his team (2021) closer to other authors such as Svensson and Oberwittler (2021) or Frøyland (2022), who are not as explicit about the boost that changes in digitalization have given to delinquency, but do recognize the impact that unstructured socialization has had on it, and do not deny that the latter may have been altered by the internet. It also adds an explicit mechanism to those of us who have advocated for a comprehensive view that combines the different aspects that change in parallel to the digitalization of society. It also adds an explicit mechanism to those of us who have pointed out the key role that digitalization and the resulting change in routines might have played in reducing crime, particularly among minors.

Because, as previously mentioned, while it is true that digitalization has affected everyone and, therefore, will have reduced the time that almost all of us spend outdoors or engaged in certain activities "in the physical world," it is not the same to reduce socialization and physical interaction with peers during adolescence and early youth as it is to reduce the socialization that occurs in stages of greater maturity. This would explain why the impact on young people is greater than on adults. Some studies on trends that have been able to compare the volume of crimes committed by young people with those committed by adults have shown that, in contrast to the decrease of the former, the rates for the latter have remained stable (see Payne et al. (2018) for a study in this regard in the Australian state of New South Wales (NSW) between 1984 and 1999). This could be due to two factors: The first is that the use of digital devices and mechanisms is higher among young people than among adults. In fact, this was at least the case in the early stages and certainly continues to be so today. The second factor to consider is that the effects might be different. In other words, spending more time at home may reduce opportunities more for young people than for adults, both due to the type of activities of the different populations and due to the variation across different life stages in the importance of unstructured socialization and the potential influence of socialization agents such as peer groups.

It is evident that these factors will have interacted with other elements commonly associated with juvenile delinquency and which have empirical support. Changes in habits will have been related to changes in public policies and in the attitudes of minors and parents and will not have acted on their own. Clearly, much more empirical research is needed on the relationship between all these factors, determining the weight that digitalization in particular may have had in changing habits and, considering the changes in it and the trend since the advent of smartphones for the digital to no longer just be at home but everywhere, about how it will influence one way or another in the future. But what can no longer be done is look the other way, ignore the correlation, and think it is a coincidence that the most important social change of our lives has nothing to do with the most powerful downward trend in crime, namely, that perpetrated by young people from the 90s to 2020. It is time to talk about the elephant in the room.

Pointing at the Elephant in the Room

Up until now, and in comparison to other more direct and explicit hypotheses focusing on the relationship between specific periods and distinct trends with more or less determined variables, the potential relationship between the process of digitalization and changes in crime trends has almost always been expressed "in a low voice," if not entirely overlooked. From the literature review conducted, it is possible to understand both why it has never been considered a strong hypothesis and why it has continued to flutter around as a plausible hypothesis.

Regarding the former, there are two fundamental reasons explaining the scarce popularity of this conjecture. On one hand, it has never been a thesis with substantial empirical support, not so much because there is a lack of data showing the correlation between the period when the process of digitalization began in the 1990s up to the present and the decrease in some forms of crime, especially juvenile delinquency, but because of the difficulty in identifying specific variables related to changes in habits due to digitalization, and even more so if it is in a causal sense. On the other hand, some misconceptions have been clarified that could have misled us regarding the true meaning of the conjecture linking digitalization with the decrease in crime. The first is the misunderstanding regarding the causal mechanism: It was never cybercrime, nor directly the internet or digitalization itself, but rather what such process caused in terms of change in minors' habits and the subsequent reduction in opportunities derived from their decreased unstructured socialization. And this also resolves the second misunderstanding related to the temporal issue: Focusing on the emergence of cybercrime, or even on the internet, as the moment from which to set the beginning of the variable, means ignoring that digitalization started earlier and with it the change in young people's habits and its consequences, which is what really has the potential to link digitalization with opportunity and this with crime.

Moreover, the literature review has also shown that the thesis linking digitalization with the crime drop has always been there, in different authors with different arguments, as something that has always fluttered among the possible explanations of the crime drop. But why did this thesis continue to hold despite the scarcity of data and misunderstandings surrounding it? One reason could be that none of the alternative or concurrent theses of the crime drop has achieved either academic consensus or sufficient empirical confirmation. But the real reason for the survival of the conjecture that is now resurging is the enormous strength of the thesis from an intuitive perspective: It is almost impossible to ignore that something that started in the 90s and continues until 2020, and is especially related to young people, is not related to the internet or, more precisely, to the process of digitalization. To put it graphically, from time to time, researchers stumbled upon the elephant in the room, and despite all being determined to ignore it, the authors of this manuscript could not stop thinking about it.

And what has changed now that makes us look the elephant directly in the eyes and start talking about it? A pandemic. The change in citizens' habits related to the increased time spent at home by certain sectors of the population usually related to delinquency could be showing us, now during the Covid-19 crisis, the elephant in the room of the change in criminal opportunities derived from a change in citizens' mobility habits. And that elephant is none other than the internet and its impact in the form of a slow and complex process of change, as is digitalization, which by affecting the mobility of many could have modified opportunities and affected crime trends. The mobility of many, but not all in the same way, but as part of a larger transformation that digitalization is producing, especially in those generations that have experienced it from its very beginnings. In fact, it has been these generations who have offered us the definitive clue.

For decades we have talked about the impact of the internet on young people's habits, its impact on their health, their academic performance, and in recent years, it has started to be related to changes in crime trends and alcohol consumption, as well as other risk behaviors. From the literature review, two different hypotheses are sought. In addition, it is also complicated to find data that directly relate digitalization with lower juvenile delinquency. But the routine activity theory (RAT) and attention to the literature on predictors of juvenile delinquency, particularly the relevance of the association between unstructured socialization (Hoeben & Weerman, 2016; Osgood et al., 1996) and delinquency, show us the indirect mechanism that could square the circle. It is true that unstructured socialization could have decreased for many other reasons, but in the task that remains to search for the specific mechanisms of such change, it seems absurd not to want to look at the role that the most important cultural change of the last 40 years, the emergence of the internet, could have played in it.

Now is the moment to acknowledge the elephant in the room and take the initial step toward developing a conjecture: to concede that there are sufficient indications to regard as plausible the notion that due to the changes in opportunities brought about by alterations in lifestyle habits, the digital technological revolution that began in the 1980s, but particularly took shape from the 1990s onwards, might have exerted multiple impacts on criminal behavior. These impacts would, in turn, have manifested themselves in varying ways across crime rates. This is the hypothesis, and its theoretical foundations in opportunity and routine activity theory (RAT) are evident. Nonetheless, there is still much work to be done. Given the abstract nature of the variable "digital technological revolution," empirically correlating it with the diverse trends of the various crimes—and acknowledging the lack of a comprehensive record of all crimes committed—presents a highly complex challenge. Yet, in order to accomplish this, and to construct the initial hypotheses that would shape the final hypothesis—further supporting them with specific empirical analyses and additional secondary studies—it was crucial to begin by highlighting what was seen by all but remained unaddressed.

References

Abrams, D. S. (2020). Covid and crime: An early empirical look. *SSRN Electronic Journal*. https://doi.org/10.2139/ssrn.3674032
Aebi, M. F. (2004). Crime trends in Western Europe from 1990 to 2000. *European Journal on Criminal Policy and Research, 10*(2–3), 163–186. https://doi.org/10.1007/s10610-004-3412-1
Aebi, M. F., & Linde, A. (2010). Is there a crime drop in Western Europe? *European Journal on Criminal Policy and Research, 16*(4), 251–277.
Aebi, M. F., & Linde, A. (2012a). Conviction statistics as an indicator of crime trends in Europe from 1990 to 2006. *European Journal on Criminal Policy and Research, 18*(1), 103–144. https://doi.org/10.1007/s10610-011-9166-7
Aebi, M. F., & Linde, A. (2012b). Crime trends in Western Europe according to official statistics from 1990 to 2007. In J. van Dijk, A. Tseloni, & G. Farrell (Eds.), *The international crime drop: New directions in research* (pp. 37–75). Palgrave Macmillan UK.
Aebi, M. F., & Linde, A. (2014). The persistence of lifestyles: Rates and correlates of homicide in Western Europe from 1960 to 2010. *European Journal of Criminology, 11*(5), 552–577. https://doi.org/10.1177/1477370814541178
Aebi, M. F., & Linde, A. (2016). Long-term trends in crime: Continuity and change. In P. Knepper & A. Johansen (Eds.), *The Oxford handbook of the history of crime and criminal justice* (pp. 57–87). Oxford University Press.

Aebi, M. F., & Tiago, M. M. (2020a). *Prisons and Prisoners in Europe in Pandemic Times: An evaluation of the medium-term impact of the COVID-19 on prison populations*. Series UNILCRIM 2020/4. Council of Europe and University of Lausanne. Open access: https://wp.unil.ch/space/publications/2199-2/

Aebi, M. F., & Tiago, M. M. (2020b). *Prisons and Prisoners in Europe in Pandemic Times: An evaluation of the short-term impact of the COVID-19 on prison populations*. Series UNILCRIM 2020/3. Council of Europe and University of Lausanne. Open access: https://wp.unil.ch/space/publications/2199-2/

Aebi, M. F., Aubusson de Cavarlay, B., Barclay, G., Gruszczynska, B., Harrendorf, S., Heiskanen, M., et al. (2010). *European Sourcebook of Crime and Criminal Justice Statistics – 2010* (4th ed.). Boom Juridische Uitgevers.

Agnew, R. (2009). *Juvenile delinquency: Causes and control* (3rd ed.). Oxford University Press.

Andersen, L. H., Anker, A. S. T., & Andersen, S. H. (2016). A formal decomposition of declining youth crime in Denmark. *Demographic Research, 35*, 1303–1316. https://doi.org/10.4054/demres.2016.35.44

Arnett, J. J. (2018). Getting better all the time: Trends in risk behavior among American adolescents since 1990. *Archives of Scientific Psychology, 6*(1), 87–95. https://doi.org/10.1037/arc0000046

Ashby, M. P. (2020). Initial evidence on the relationship between the coronavirus pandemic and crime in the United States. *Crime Science, 9*(1), 1–16. https://doi.org/10.1186/s40163-020-00117-6

Austin, J., Clear, T., & Rosenfeld, R. (2019). Explaining the past and projecting future crime rates. HFG. (2021, August 1). Retrieved August 11, 2022, from https://www.hfg.org/hfg_reports/explaining-the-past-and-projecting-future-crime-rates/

Ball, J., et al. (2022). The great decline in adolescent risk behaviours: Unitary trend, separate trends, or cascade? *Social Science & Medicine*, 115616.

Ball, J., et al. (2023). Understanding youth drinking decline: Similarity and change in the function and social meaning of alcohol use (and non-use) in adolescent cohorts 20 years apart. *Drug and Alcohol Review*.

Baumer, E. P., & Wolff, K. T. (2014). The breadth and causes of contemporary cross-national homicide trends. *Crime and Justice, 43*(1), 231–287.

Baumer, E. P., Vélez, M. B., & Rosenfeld, R. (2018). Bringing crime trends back into criminology: A critical assessment of the literature and a blueprint for future inquiry. *Annual Review of Criminology, 1*(1), 39–61.

Baumer, E. P., Cundiff, K., & Luo, L. (2021). The contemporary transformation of American youth: An analysis of change in the prevalence of delinquency, 1991–2015. *Criminology, 59*(1), 109–136.

Beerthuizen, M. G. C. J., Weijters, G., & van der Laan, A. M. (2017). The release of Grand Theft Auto V and registered juvenile crime in the Netherlands. *European Journal of Criminology, 14*(6), 751–765. https://doi.org/10.1177/1477370817717070

Berghuis, B., & de Waard, J. (2017). Verdampende jeugdcriminaliteit: Verklaringen van deinternationale daling. *Justitiële Verkenningen, 43*, 10–27.

Berlin, I. (1953). *The philosophy of the enlightenment*.

Blumstein, A., & Farrington, D. (2000). In A. Blumstein & J. Wallman (Eds.), *The crime drop in America* (pp. 13–44). Cambridge University Press.

Blumstein, A., & Rosenfeld, R. (2008, December). Factors contributing to US crime trends. In *Understanding crime trends: Workshop report* (Vol. 2, pp. 13–44). National Academies Press.

Braudel, F. (1958, December). Histoire et sciences sociales: la longue durée. In *Annales. Histoire, Sciences Sociales* (Vol. 13, 4, pp. 725-753). Cambridge University Press.

Breuer, J., Vogelgesang, J., Quandt, T., & Festl, R. (2015). *Violent video games and physical aggression: Evidence for a selection effect among adolescents* (Vol. 4, No. 4, p. 305). Educational Publishing Foundation.

Buil-Gil, D., Miró-Llinares, F., Moneva, A., Kemp, S., & Díaz-Castaño, N. (2020). Cybercrime and shifts in opportunities during COVID-19: A preliminary analysis in the UK. *European Societies, 23*(sup1), S47–S59. https://doi.org/10.1080/14616696.2020.1804973

Button, M., & Cross, C. (2017). *Cyber frauds, scams and their victims*. Routledge.
Caneppele, S., & Aebi, M. F. (2019). Crime drop or police recording flop? on the relationship between the decrease of offline crime and the increase of online and hybrid crimes. *Policing: A Journal of Policy and Practice, 13*(1), 66–79. https://doi.org/10.1093/police/pax055
Carpenter, C. S., Kloska, D. D., O'Malley, P., & Johnston, L. (2007). Alcohol control policies and youth alcohol consumption: Evidence from 28 years of monitoring the future. *The B.E. Journal of Economic Analysis & Policy, 7*(1), 1–21. https://doi.org/10.2202/1935-1682.1637
Chomynová, P., & Kážmér, L. (2019). Leisure-time socializing with peers as a mediator of recent decline in alcohol use in Czech adolescents. *Journal of Substance Use, 24*(6), 630–637. https://doi.org/10.1080/14659891.2019.1640304
Cohen, L. E., & Felson, M. (1979). Social Change and crime rate trends: A routine activity approach. *American Sociological Review, 44*(4), 588. https://doi.org/10.2307/2094589
Easttom, C., Taylor, J., & Hurley, H. (2011). *Computer crime, investigation, and the law*. Course Technology.
Eisner, M. (2008). Modernity strikes back? A historical perspective on the latest increase in interpersonal violence (1960–1990). *International Journal of Conflict and Violence, 2*(2), 288–316. https://doi.org/10.4119/ijcv-2769
Elias, N., & Hammer, H. (1939). *über den Prozeß der Zivilisation*. Suhrkamp.
Elonheimo, H. (2014). Evidence for the crime drop: Survey findings from two Finnish cities between 1992 and 2013. *Journal of Scandinavian Studies in Criminology and Crime Prevention, 15*(2), 209–217.
Estrada, F. (2019). Youth and crime in a welfare state. Trends, inequalities and societal response. In J. Lunneblad (Ed.), *Policing schools: School violence and the juridification of youth. Young people and learning processes in school and everyday life* (Vol. 2). Springer. https://doi.org/10.1007/978-3-030-18605-0_3
Estrada, F., Bäckman, O., & Nilsson, A. (2016). The darker side of equality? The declining gender gap in crime: Historical trends and an enhanced analysis of staggered birth cohorts. *The British Journal of Criminology, 56*(6), 1272–1290. https://doi.org/10.1093/bjc/azv114
Farrall, S. (2017). Outlining the crime drop. In *Re-examining the crime drop* (pp. 1–8). Palgrave Macmillan.
Farrell, G. (2013). Five tests for a theory of the crime drop. *Crime Science, 2*(1), 1–8. https://doi.org/10.1186/2193-7680-2-5
Farrell, G., & Birks, D. (2018). Did cybercrime cause the crime drop? *Crime Science, 7*(1), 1–4. https://doi.org/10.1186/s40163-018-0082-8
Farrell, G., & Birks, D. (2020). Further rejection of the cybercrime hypothesis. *Crime Science, 9*(1). https://doi.org/10.1186/s40163-020-00113-w
Farrell, G., Tseloni, A., Mailley, J., & Tilley, N. (2011). The crime drop and the security hypothesis. *Journal of Research in Crime and Delinquency, 48*(2), 147–175. https://doi.org/10.1177/0022427810391539
Farrell, G., Tilley, N., & Tseloni, A. (2014). Why the crime drop? *Crime and Justice, 43*(1), 421–490. https://doi.org/10.1086/678081
Farrell, G., Laycock, G., & Tilley, N. (2015). Debuts and legacies: The crime drop and the role of adolescence-limited and persistent offending. *Crime Science, 4*(1), 1–10. https://doi.org/10.1186/s40163-015-0028-3
Farrington, D. P. (2003). Developmental and life-course criminology: Key theoretical and empirical issues-the 2002 sutherland award address*. *Criminology, 41*(2), 221–225. https://doi.org/10.1111/j.1745-9125.2003.tb00987.x
Felson, R. B., & Staff, J. (2010). The effects of alcohol intoxication on violent versus other offending. *Criminal Justice and Behavior, 37*(12), 1343–1360. https://doi.org/10.1177/0093854810382003
Felson, R., Savolainen, J., Aaltonen, M., & Moustgaard, H. (2008). Is the association between alcohol use and delinquency causal or spurious? *Criminology, 46*(3), 785–808. https://doi.org/10.1111/j.1745-9125.2008.00120.x
Felson, M., Jiang, S., & Xu, Y. (2020). Routine activity effects of the Covid-19 pandemic on burglary in Detroit, March, 2020. *Crime Science, 9*(1), 1–7.

Ferguson, C. J. (2015). Do angry birds make for angry children? A meta-analysis of video game influences on children's and adolescents' aggression, mental health, prosocial behavior, and academic performance. *Perspectives on Psychological Science, 10*(5), 646–666. https://doi.org/10.1177/1745691615592234

Fernández-Molina, E., & Bartolomé Gutiérrez, R. (2018). Juvenile crime drop: What is happening with youth in Spain and why? *European Journal of Criminology, 17*(3), 306–331. https://doi.org/10.1177/1477370818792383

Frøyland, L. R. (2022). Understanding societal trends in adolescent violence. *Nordisk Tidsskrift for Kriminalvidenskab, 109*(1), 53–59. https://doi.org/10.7146/ntfk.v109i1.130288

Ganpat, S. M., Garius, L., Tseloni, A., & Tilley, N. (2020). Violence and the crime drop. *European Journal of Criminology, 1477370820913456.*

Graham, A., Kulig, T. C., & Cullen, F. T. (2019). Willingness to report crime to the police. *Policing: An International Journal, 43*(1), 1–16. https://doi.org/10.1108/pijpsm-07-2019-0115

Green, D. A. (2016). A funny thing happened on the way to mass subjugation: Propensity, opportunity, and irony in two accounts of the crime decline. *Dialectical Anthropology, 40*, 363–376. https://doi.org/10.1007/s10624-016-9438-1

Griffiths, G., & Norris, G. (2020). Explaining the crime drop: Contributions to declining crime rates from youth cohorts since 2005. *Crime, Law and Social Change, 73*(1), 25–53.

Grucza, R. A., Sher, K. J., Kerr, W. C., Krauss, M. J., Lui, C. K., McDowell, Y. E., et al. (2018). Trends in adult alcohol use and binge drinking in the early 21st-century United States: A meta-analysis of 6 National Survey Series. *Alcoholism: Clinical and Experimental Research, 42*(10), 1939–1950.

Halford, E., Dixon, A., Farrell, G., Malleson, N., & Tilley, N. (2020). Crime and coronavirus: Social distancing, lockdown and the mobility elasticity of crime. *Crime Science.* https://doi.org/10.31235/osf.io/4qzca

Hebenton, B., & Jou, S. (2018). Criminology in China. In R. A. Triplett (Ed.), *The handbook of the history and philosophy of criminology* (pp. 377–391). Wiley.

Hindelang, M. J., Gottfredson, M. R., & Garofalo, J. (1978). *Victims of personal crime: An empirical foundation for a theory of personal victimization.* Ballinger.

Hoar, S. B. (2005). Trends in cybercrime: The dark side of the internet. *Criminal Justice, 20*, 4.

Hodgkinson, T., & Andresen, M. A. (2020). Show me a man or a woman alone and I'll show you a saint: Changes in the frequency of criminal incidents during the covid-19 pandemic. *Journal of Criminal Justice, 69*, 101706. https://doi.org/10.1016/j.jcrimjus.2020.101706

Hoeben, E. M., & Weerman, F. M. (2016). Why is involvement in unstructured socializing related to adolescent delinquency? *Criminology, 54*(2), 242–281. https://doi.org/10.1111/1745-9125.12105

Hoeben, E. M., Meldrum, R. C., Walker, D. A., & Young, J. T. (2016). The role of peer delinquency and unstructured socializing in explaining delinquency and substance use: A state-of-the-art review. *Journal of Criminal Justice, 47*, 108–122. https://doi.org/10.1016/j.jcrimjus.2016.08.001

Humphreys, L., Francis, B., & McVie, S. (2014). *Understanding the crime drop in Scotland.* AQMeN Research Briefing 1.

Hunt, D. (2017). *How large changes in the functioning economy effect crime rates in America: A national examination of the less cash–less crime paradigm.*

Jehle, J.-M., & Harrendorf, S. (Eds.). (2010). *Defining and registering criminal offences and measures: Standards for a European comparison.* Göttingen Studies in Criminal Law and Justice 10. Universitätsverlag Göttingen. Open access: https://library.oapen.org/handle/20.500.12657/32614

Johnson, S., & Nikolovska, M. (2022). The effect of covid-19 restrictions on routine activities and online crime. *Journal of Quantitative Criminology.* https://doi.org/10.31235/osf.io/ze49b

Kaakinen, M., & Näsi, M. (2021). Nuorisorikollisuuden esiintyvyys ja tekomäärät Suomessa 1995–2020. *Kriminologia, 1*(1), 5–19.

Kemp, S., Miró-Llinares, F., & Moneva, A. (2020). The dark figure and the cyber fraud rise in Europe: Evidence from Spain. *European Journal on Criminal Policy and Research, 26*(3), 293–312. https://doi.org/10.1007/s10610-020-09439-2

Kemp, S., Buil-Gil, D., Moneva, A., Miró-Llinares, F., & Díaz-Castaño, N. (2021). Empty streets, busy internet. A time series analysis of cybercrime and fraud trends during COVID-19. *Journal of Contemporary Criminal Justice.* https://doi.org/10.31235/osf.io/38wfy

Kerr, J. D. (2005). *Crime rates and the technological transformation of leisure: A routine activities approach.* University of Kentucky.

Keyes, K. M., Schulenberg, J. E., O'Malley, P. M., Johnston, L. D., Bachman, J. G., Li, G., & Hasin, D. (2012). Birth cohort effects on adolescent alcohol use: The influence of social norms from 1976 to 2007. *Archives of General Psychiatry, 69*(12), 1304–1313.

Keyes, K. M., Gary, D. S., Beardslee, J., Prins, S. J., O'Malley, P. M., Rutherford, C., & Schulenberg, J. (2018). Joint effects of age, period, and cohort on conduct problems among American adolescents from 1991 through 2015. *American Journal of Epidemiology, 187*(3), 548–557.

Killias, M. (2006). The opening and closing of breaches. *European Journal of Criminology, 3*(1), 11–31. https://doi.org/10.1177/1477370806059079

Killias, M., & Aebi, M. F. (2000). Crime Trends in Europe from 1990 to 1996: How Europe illustrates the limits of the American experience. *European Journal on Criminal Policy and Research, 8*(1), 43–63.

Kim, J., Bushway, S., & Tsao, H. S. (2016). Identifying classes of explanations for crime drop: Period and cohort effects for New York State. *Journal of Quantitative Criminology, 32*(3), 357–375.

Kivivuori, J., & Bernburg, J. G. (2011). Delinquency research in the Nordic countries. *Crime and Justice, 40*(1), 405–477.

Knepper, P. (2018). Second science? The future of historical science in criminology. In *Realist Evaluation for Crime Science* (pp. 119–137). https://doi.org/10.4324/9781315627144-8

Kotkin, J. (2002). *The new geography: how the digital revolution is reshaping the American landscape.* Random House.

Linde, A., & Aebi, M. F. (2020). La criminologie comparée à l'heure de la société numérique: Les théories traditionnelles peuvent-elles expliquer les tendances de la cyber-délinquance ? *Revue Internationale de Criminologie et de Police Technique et Scientifique, 73*(4), 387–414.

Matthews, B., & Minton, J. (2018). Rethinking one of criminology's 'brute facts': The age–crime curve and the crime drop in Scotland. *European journal of criminology, 15*(3), 296–320.

McCaffree, K., & Proctor, K. R. (2017). Cocooned from crime: The relationship between video games and Crime. *Society, 55*(1), 41–52. https://doi.org/10.1007/s12115-017-0211-0

McGuire, M., & Dowling, S. (2013). Cyber crime: A review of the evidence. *Summary of key findings and implications. Home Office Research report, 75*, 1–35.

Meldrum, R. C., & Leimberg, A. (2018). Unstructured socializing with peers and risk of substance use: Where does the risk begin? *Journal of Drug Issues, 48*(3), 452–471. https://doi.org/10.1177/0022042618774263

Miró, F., & Johnson, S. (2017). Cybercrime and place: Applying environmental criminology to crimes in cyberspace.

Miró-Llinares, F. (2012). *El cibercrimen: Fenomenología y criminología de la delincuencia en el ciberespacio. El cibercrimen.*

Miró-Llinares, F. (2021). Crimen, cibercrimen y covid-19: Desplazamiento (acelerado) de Oportunidades y Adaptación situacional de Ciberdelitos *IDP. Revista De Internet Derecho y Política,* (32). https://doi.org/10.7238/idp.v0i32.373815

Miró-Llinares, F., & Moneva, A. (2019). What about cyberspace (and cybercrime alongside it)? A reply to Farrell and Birks "did cybercrime cause the crime drop? *Crime Science, 8*(1). https://doi.org/10.1186/s40163-019-0107-y

Mohler, G., Bertozzi, A. L., Carter, J., Short, M. B., Sledge, D., Tita, G. E., Uchida, C. D., & Brantingham, P. J. (2020). Impact of social distancing during COVID-19 pandemic on crime in Los Angeles and Indianapolis. *Journal of Criminal Justice, 68*, 101692. https://doi.org/10.1016/j.jcrimjus.2020.101692

Moss, S. L., Santaella-Tenorio, J., Mauro, P. M., Keyes, K. M., & Martins, S. S. (2019). Changes over time in marijuana use, deviant behavior and preference for risky behavior among US adolescents from 2002 to 2014: Testing the moderating effect of gender and age. *Addiction, 114*(4), 674–686. https://doi.org/10.1111/add.14506

Osgood, D. W., & Anderson, A. L. (2004). Unstructured socializing and rates of delinquency. *Criminology., 42*, 519–550.

Osgood, D. W., Wilson, J. K., O'Malley, P. M., Bachman, J. G., & Johnston, L. D. (1996). Routine activities and individual deviant behavior. *American Sociological Review, 61*(4), 635–655. https://doi.org/10.2307/2096397

Parker, D. B. (1989). Computer crime: Criminal justice resource manual.

Parker, D. B., & Nycum, S. H. (1984). Computer crime. *Communications of the ACM, 27*(4), 313–315.

Payne, J., & Morgan, A. (2020). *COVID-19 and violent crime: A comparison of recorded offence rates and dynamic forecasts (ARIMA) for March 2020 in Queensland, Australia.* A preprint. https://osf.io/preprints/socarxiv/g4kh7

Payne, J., Brown, R., & Broadhurst, R. (2018). Where have all the young offenders gone? Examining changes in offending between two NSW birth cohorts. *Trends and Issues in Crime and Criminal Justice, 553*, 1–15. Australian Institute of Criminology. https://www.aic.gov.au/publications/tandi/tandi553

Payne, J. L., Morgan, A., & Piquero, A. R. (2020). *Covid-19 and social distancing measures in Queensland Australia are associated with short-term decreases in recorded violent crime.* https://doi.org/10.31235/osf.io/z4m8t

Pease, K. (2003). Crime futures and foresight: Challenging criminal behaviour in the information age. In *Crime and the Internet* (pp. 30–40). Routledge.

Pinker, S. (2011). *The better angels of our nature: Why violence has declined.* Viking.

Piquero, A. R., Riddell, J. R., Bishopp, S. A., Narvey, C., Reid, J. A., & Piquero, N. L. (2020). Staying home, staying safe? A short-term analysis of COVID-19 on Dallas domestic violence. *American Journal of Criminal Justice, 45*(4), 601–635. https://doi.org/10.1007/s12103-020-09531-7

Polglase, L., & Lambie, I. (2023). A sharp decline in youth crime: reviewing trends in New Zealand's youth offending rates between 1998 and 2019. *Current Issues in Criminal Justice*, 1–21.

Popovici, I., Homer, J. F., Fang, H., & French, M. T. (2012). Alcohol use and crime: Findings from a longitudinal sample of US adolescents and young adults. *Alcoholism: Clinical and Experimental Research, 36*(3), 532–543. https://doi.org/10.1111/j.1530-0277.2011.01641.x

Pridemore, W. A., Roche, S. P., & Rogers, M. L. (2018). Cashlessness and street crime: A cross-national study of direct deposit payment and robbery rates. *Justice Quarterly, 35*(5), 919–939. https://doi.org/10.1080/07418825.2018.1424923

Rosenfeld, R. (2018). Studying crime trends: Normal science and exogenous shocks*. *Criminology, 56*(1), 5–26. https://doi.org/10.1111/1745-9125.12170

Rosenfeld, R., & Weisburd, D. (2016). Explaining recent crime trends: Introduction to the special issue. *Journal of Quantitative Criminology, 32*(3), 329–334. https://doi.org/10.1007/s10940-016-9317-6

Rossow, I., Pape, H., & Torgersen, L. (2020). Decline in adolescent drinking: Some possible explanations. *Drug and alcohol review, 39*(6), 721–728.

Sakalauskas, G., Kalpokas, V., Buzaitytė-Kašalynienė, J., & Švedaitė-Sakalauskė, B. (2021). International comparison of manifestations and tendencies of registered juvenile delinquency in Lithuania. *Kriminologijos studijos, 9*, 173–198.

Salmi, V. (2009). Self-reported juvenile delinquency in Finland 1995–2008 (English Summary. Research Report No. 246). National Research Institute of Legal Policy.

Sampson, R. J., & Laub, J. H. (2003). Desistance from crime over the life course. In *Handbook of the life course* (pp. 295–309). Springer.

Shen, Y., Fu, R., & Noguchi, H. (2021). COVID-19's lockdown and crime victimization: The state of emergency under the Abe administration. *Asian Economic Policy Review, 16*(2), 327–348.

Sivertsson, F., Nilsson, A., & Bäckman, O. (2019). Participation and frequency in criminal convictions across 25 successive birth cohorts: Collectivity, polarization, or convergence? *Justice Quarterly*. https://doi.org/10.1080/07418825.2019.1699941

Svensson, R., & Oberwittler, D. (2021). Changing routine activities and the decline of youth crime: A repeated cross-sectional analysis of self-reported delinquency in Sweden, 1999–2017. *Criminology, 59*(2), 351–386. https://doi.org/10.1111/1745-9125.12273

Svensson, R., & Ring, J. (2007). Trends in self-reported youth crime and victimisation in Sweden, 1995–2005. *Journal of Scandinavian Studies in Criminology and Crime Prevention, 8*(2), 153–177. https://doi.org/10.1080/14043850701517805

Tcherni, M., Davies, A., Lopes, G., & Lizotte, A. (2015). The dark figure of online property crime: Is cyberspace hiding a crime wave? *Justice Quarterly, 33*(5), 890–911. https://doi.org/10.1080/07418825.2014.994658

Thompson, R. (2014). *Understanding theft from the person and robbery of personal property victimisation trends in England and Wales, 1994–2010/11*. Nottingham Trent University (United Kingdom).

Tilley, N., Farrell, G., & Clarke, R. V. (2015a). *Target suitability and the crime drop*. Essay, Palgrave Macmillan UK.

Tilley, N., Thompson, R., Farrell, G., Grove, L., & Tseloni, A. (2015b). Do burglar alarms increase burglary risk? A counter-intuitive finding and possible explanations. *Crime Prevention and Community Safety, 17*(1), 1–19. https://doi.org/10.1057/cpcs.2014.17

Tseloni, A., Thompson, R., Grove, L., Tilley, N., & Farrell, G. (2017). The effectiveness of burglary security devices. *Security Journal, 30*(2), 646–664. https://doi.org/10.1057/sj.2014.30

Twenge, J. M. (2017). *iGen: Why today's super-connected kids are growing up less rebellious, more tolerant, less happy--and completely unprepared for adulthood--and what that means for the rest of us*. Atria Books.

Van der Laan, A. M., Rokven, J., Weijters, G., & Beerthuizen, M. G. (2019). The drop in juvenile delinquency in the Netherlands: Changes in exposure to risk and protection. *Justice Quarterly*, 1–21. https://doi.org/10.1080/07418825.2019.1656762

Van der Laan, A. M., et al. (2021). The drop in juvenile delinquency in the Netherlands: Changes in exposure to risk and protection. *Justice Quarterly, 38*(3), 433–453.

Van Dijk, J., & Tseloni, A. (2012). Global overview: International trends in victimization and recorded crime. In *The international crime drop* (pp. 11–36).

Vashishtha, R., Holmes, J., Pennay, A., Dietze, P. M., & Livingston, M. (2022). An examination of the role of changes in country-level leisure time internet use and computer gaming on adolescent drinking in 33 European countries. *International Journal of Drug Policy, 100*, 103508. https://doi.org/10.1016/j.drugpo.2021.103508

Vasiljevic, Z., Svensson, R., & Shannon, D. (2020). Immigration and crime: A time-trend analysis of self-reported crime in Sweden, 1999–2017. *Nordic Journal of Criminology, 21*(1), 1–10. https://doi.org/10.1080/2578983X.2019.1688955

Wall, D. (2007). *Cybercrime: The transformation of crime in the information age* (Vol. 4).

Ward, M. R. (2011). Video games and crime. *Contemporary Economic Policy, 29*(2), 261–273. https://doi.org/10.1111/j.1465-7287.2010.00216.x

White, G. F., Gainey, R. R., & Triplett, R. A. (2015). Alcohol outlets and neighborhood crime: A longitudinal analysis. *Crime & Delinquency, 61*(6), 851–872. https://doi.org/10.1177/0011128712466386

Williams, M. L., & Levi, M. (2017). Cybercrime prevention. In *Handbook of crime prevention and community safety* (pp. 454–469). Routledge.

Wright, R., Tekin, E., Topalli, V., McClellan, C., Dickinson, T., & Rosenfeld, R. (2017). Less cash, less crime: Evidence from the Electronic Benefit Transfer Program. *The Journal of Law and Economics, 60*(2), 361–383. https://doi.org/10.1086/693745

Zimring, W. D. S. F. E. (2006). *The great American crime decline*. Oxford University Press.

Open Access This chapter is licensed under the terms of the Creative Commons Attribution 4.0 International License (http://creativecommons.org/licenses/by/4.0/), which permits use, sharing, adaptation, distribution and reproduction in any medium or format, as long as you give appropriate credit to the original author(s) and the source, provide a link to the Creative Commons license and indicate if changes were made.

The images or other third party material in this chapter are included in the chapter's Creative Commons license, unless indicated otherwise in a credit line to the material. If material is not included in the chapter's Creative Commons license and your intended use is not permitted by statutory regulation or exceeds the permitted use, you will need to obtain permission directly from the copyright holder.

Chapter 4
Crime Opportunities, Lockdowns, and Online Video Games: The Digital Leisure Hypothesis (and More on the Impact of Digitalization on Crime Trends)

Fernando Miró-Llinares

On Lockdown and Its Consequences

As a natural social experiment which is currently occurring all around the world in different circumstances and scope, the crisis of the Covid-19 pandemic constitutes an undeniable scientific opportunity for social investigation (Sticke & Felson, 2020). Since some variables, typically studied because of their link to crime, have become isolated or modified in hitherto unobserved conditions, studying the pandemic's impact on delinquency can help us understand what is happening and be prepared for what is yet to come. The fact that other pandemics and social crises in the past have been derived from similar events and that their effects on delinquency have been measured (see Cromwell et al., 1995; LeBeau, 2002; and more recently Jenkins & Phillips, 2008; and Verano et al., 2010 regarding the effects of Hurricane Katrina) opens up the possibility of using the past as a way of anticipating the future and predicting consequences of current crises in crime (Stickle & Felson, 2020). Moreover, analyzing the impact of the pandemic and lockdown on crime rates can contribute to explaining past events and trends: by observing current events and understanding the causal significance of previously disregarded or underestimated variables, a clearer delineation of historical traces, trends, and causes of delinquency can be achieved. In the study of the Covid-19 crisis from a social perspective, Braudel's advice to prioritize plural time over singular time (1958) is followed. This approach helps to avoid being solely influenced by the rapid pace of historical

---

This chapter has been possible thanks to the grand PROGRAMA PROMETEO 2023- CIPROM/2022/33 offered by the Generalitat Valenciana.

F. Miró-Llinares (✉)
Crimina Center, University Miguel Hernández of Elche, Elche, Spain
e-mail: f.miro@crimina.es

events and emphasizes "la longue durée," the time determined by natural and tangible factors. Current times change slowly and subtly, which can obscure the magnitude of change, despite its real existence.

Concerning the research question, the most abrupt and evident change during the pandemic was the impact of mobility restrictions and social distancing on delinquency. The analysis of the impact of both Covid-19 and the different kinds of lockdown on crime rates has shown the relevance of factors such as opportunity and changes in mobility in the latest crime trends. Many studies have linked mobility restrictions during the most intense moments of the pandemic to a decrease in urban delinquency (see Nivette et al., 2021, for England; Kirchmaier & Villa-Llera, 2020; Agrawal et al., 2022; for New Zealand, Cheung and Gurnby; for Mexico, Estevez-Soto, 2019; in Sweden, Gerell et al., 2020) with just a few exceptions of unaffected crime types. Public disorder and drug dealing did not decrease, in the cases of both England (Kirchmaier & Villa-Lera, 2020) and Australia (Kim & Leung, 2020), probably as a result of greater police presence to enforce lockdown rules and hence more ample controls. Online fraud and other types of cybercrime did not decrease either (Agrawal et al., 2022). Most studies analyzing the evolution of crime during the pandemic certify a decrease in different crime types during the lockdown (Abrams, 2021) and that it happened in different moments across countries coinciding with the application of movement restrictions. Furthermore, varying lockdown intensity and differences in restrictive measures may also have influenced the intensity in the decrease of crime in general (Riddell et al., 2021; Reid & Baglivio, 2022; Nivette et al., 2021; or in specific crime typologies, particularly youth crime, McCarthy et al., 2021).

Behind all these investigations, one variable stands out: mobility. Just like some have accurately claimed under the idea of "the mobility elasticity of crime" (Halford et al., 2020), the changes to mobility were the primary cause of a shift in the rates of many types of crime, especially during the early stages of the pandemic. Later studies, focused on the analysis of what happened during the different lockdowns and when restrictions began to de-escalate and mobility went back to normal rates, show how the loosening of the restrictions led to a gradual increase in crime (Langton et al., 2020; López & Rosenfeld, 2021; crime, quarantine), which not only supports the routine activity approach (López & Rosenfeld, 2021) in showing the impact of changes in everyday activities on crime (Cheung & Gunby, 2021) but also points to a much more specific direction of habit changes: the idea that spending more time at home, in this case due to the lockdown, decreases crime (Díaz et al., 2021; López & Rosenfeld, 2021). This is not a matter of how mobility affects crime rates but of how less time spent in the streets, and hence less frequent convergence with potential offenders, affects crime rates. Another abrupt change was the digital boom regarding everyday activities such as shopping or remote work. The most recent investigations suggest that an increase in the time spent at home may have also increased the number of victims of online shopping scams and other cybercrimes (Miró-Llinares, 2021; Buil-Gil et al., 2020; Kemp et al., 2021; Buil-Gil & Zeng, 2021; Khweiled et al., 2021; Buil-Gil et al., 2021; Johnson & Nikolovska, 2022, all for the UK, and Lallie et al., 2021 for China).

Beyond the undeniable criminological interest of these changes in the short term, and the statement of their impact on crime tendencies, however, crime trends are studied to understand both events and variables. To this end, it is useful to consider Braudel's caveat, namely, understanding that observations during the pandemic are not isolated in time but that they are embedded in the slow and sustained process of the digital revolution, which has been taking place for decades and became more visible and acute during the Covid-19 crisis. In this context, it is clear that both crime opportunities and crime were already affected, since some of the changes during the Covid-19 crisis had already been taking place and social habits had been changing for decades already (Aebi & Linde, 2010; Miró-Llinares & Moneva, 2019). From this broader perspective, the pandemic not only brings about the opportunity to analyze the immediate social change provoked by digital advances and their effects on the prevalence of internet delinquency (Buil-Gil et al., 2021; Kemp et al., 2021), but it also allows us to look into crime trends of the past, using data from the present, and reconsider the impact that different stages of digitalization may have had on crime. Covid-19 has made it impossible to ignore the impact of digitalization and has come to prove that mobility determines opportunity which, in turn, determines crime. This chapter aims to determine whether this mechanism has been gradually influencing crime rates over an extended period.

This chapter starts from a common presumption about events in the recent past, namely, the impact of abrupt changes in mobility on crime opportunities and, subsequently, crime rates. It analyzes how the first three decades of digitalization may have affected, and will continue to affect, the evolution of delinquency. The question is, what if the determining factor for changes in these slow and irregular trends was also a slow and irregular change in the lifestyles of citizens and the criminal opportunities derived from it? Changes in the habits of citizens, that is more time spent at home, at least in certain portions of the population, and the link of this circumstance to shifts in crime rates during the Covid-19 crisis may be indicative of the elephant in the room: the impact of citizens' mobility habits on criminal opportunity. This elephant does not come in the form of abrupt changes exclusively but also exists as a slow and complex process of changes such as digitalization, which may have affected both crime opportunities and trends as a consequence of changing mobility for many citizens.

Compared to other, more direct and explicit hypotheses centered around the relationship between specific periods and trends with relatively strictly defined variables, the potential connection between processes of digitalization and changes in crime has been largely underexplored. Many authors do grant that the current technological revolution must have had considerable effects on crime, but few have pointed them out explicitly. The first steps here will be connecting the digital revolution to changes in crime opportunities, stating the abundance of hints at the possibility that changes in opportunities are a result of shifts in life habits, resulting in multiple effects on delinquency. The second step is to admit that this conjecture needs refinement and that it is enormously complex to test, given the fuzziness of the variable "digitalization" and the abundance of known and hitherto unknown possible effects on crime.

This chapter is therefore not testing a hypothesis but elaborating a theoretical base that allows the previously developed conjecture to be sustained more explicitly, such that specific trends and hypotheses can be embedded in a common framework. The initial hypotheses will be supported by secondary empirical analyses. Therefore, the first section of this chapter will establish the analytical background to support the conjecture described above. This requires redressing arguments against the connection between the crime drop of past decades and digital technology, shedding light on some misunderstandings. The subsequent section will clarify the concept of the digital revolution to help us build better conjectures and concrete hypotheses. The final section deals with the specific mechanisms behind exemplary changes in crime trends.

One Digital Revolution, One Crime Trend, One Micro Mechanism, or Many of Them? Analytical Decomposition of the Bases of the Conjecture

In historical, sociological, and criminological analysis, it is common to group events, occurrences, and periods of multiple and varied social impacts into broader frameworks that encompass them in a category to describe their aggregate impact. This also allows for a more in-depth analysis of differences and commonalities that broaden our understanding of such events and helps us obtain scope. However, this may come at the expense of losing focus on the specific effect of each phenomenon and the meaning of the causal connection between specific events. An analytical approach would therefore recommend defragmentation whenever possible, that is, ungrouping events and focusing analysis on them with an explanatory intention, despite having to add them back later and accept their complexity. This applies to the question of the social effects and consequences of what this book has holistically termed "digitalization" on phenomena that are broadly collected under the term "crime."

Research on the crime drop in past decades has suggested that the decrease in criminal offenses against property perpetrated by adolescents and young adults may be a result of changes in life habits. Such changes include longer time spent at home related to video gaming, a shift toward digital leisure, or the progressive substitution of cash money (Miró-Llinares & Moneva, 2019; Aebi & Linde, 2010; Kerr, 2005). The goal of last chapter was to inquire why the conjecture on digital transformation and crime, even it may represent one of the main explanations for some recent changes in crime trends, has not yet had significant academic success. And it was suggested, trying to solve one of the misunderstandings surrounding the meaning and scope of the relationship between cybercrime and crime drop, that cybercrime itself does not transform or reduce criminal opportunities by increasing leisure and other activities at home. Rather, it is digitalization, particularly since the advent of the internet, that has had this effect. It is the opportunity, in this case, provided by the digitalization process that creates a connection between two apparently independent trends. This more accurate identification of the core of the hypothesis also serves to refute a supposed temporal inconsistency (Farrell & Birks, 2018). Digitalization had already arrived in the 80s and proliferated especially in the mid to late 90s and was already affecting, along with other changes in leisure, the time that young people spent at home and subsequently the crime opportunities that this entailed. But the conjecture needs to be segregated into specific hypotheses, and this is the place to do it.

This chapter holds the general conjectural idea that the digital revolution of the past 30+ years would have affected crime by modifying the criminal opportunities (old and new) for convergence of aggressors and victims in places of crime and that this has been reflected in crime trends. The advantage of such a general consideration is that it is difficult to rebut; the disadvantage, however, is that, as it stands, it is difficult to test. When overly broad descriptions are included in a conjecture, the analysis ends up conflating events, causes, and timelines that may be distinct or lacking consideration of their specific contexts. This makes the hypothesis both irrefutable and untestable.

Constructing a testable conjecture, therefore, requires the decomposition of its elements, which is what the present section is aimed at. The section starts narrowing down the term digitalization, pointing out its main stages in terms of social impact, and connecting them to the possible causal mechanisms of the connection between digitalization, criminal opportunity, and delinquency. The latter will be broken down into criminal modalities on the one hand and into typologies of aggressors and victims on the other hand. This chapter will not provide a complete analysis for each of the specific developments of digitalization but focus on the most relevant changes that most clearly show causal mechanisms that link digitalization and crime trends. More work is left to future investigations, elucidating the concrete connection of each technological development with social change and crime trends, since many more connections between a concept as broad as the digital revolution and a phenomenon are to be expected. Hence, we cannot add too general of a description to the analysis without risking to treat different events, causes, and points in time without due consideration of their particular contexts. Our conjecture would thus end up untestable, as well as incontestable.

It is undeniable that many of the social changes of recent years are part of a broad and complex process that, as Kotkin (2002) pointed out, means both an acceleration of the way information is processed and disseminated and a transformation of the meaning of how people and communities communicate across the dimensions of space and time. The technological revolution that derived from the creation of personal computers, the internet, and smartphones already began in the late 1960s and early 1970s and has continued to the present. Since Charles Kline sent a text message from a computer at UCLA to another at Stanford on October 29, 1969, this process has sparked a technological explosion that has transformed society, akin to few other technological evolutions before it. The creation of the largest information and communication network in human history, the internet, lies at the heart of this informational earthquake. Amid such a revolution, where it appears we are still navigating its initial stages, comprehensively reflecting on and structuring this evolutionary period is exceedingly complex. This challenge does not stem from an inability to pinpoint major milestones in the shift toward our digital society but rather from the ongoing difficulty in assessing the significance of emerging technologies that have only just begun to reshape our lives and will undoubtedly continue to do so in the future.

Considering the impact that different digital technologies could have had on society, both in terms of the emergence of new values and interests, and the changes in social habits that could lead to criminal opportunities, however, it is consensual to state that, although digitalization had already begun in the 1960s, it wasn't until the 1980s and early 1990s that the first effects of this revolution began to be apparent. It is via the popularization of the personal computer, used first in the business environment and later in homes, that digitalization had an impact on everyday life and, along with it, on crime. The appearance of new objects of value and interest such as computer systems and computer data marks the first stage of this evolution, although at the time it was hard to inflict massive damage to data. Terminals were few and far between and attacks had to be perpetrated in the physical space, as opposed to later remote hacks. However, it was during that time that a fundamental aspect of what we now recognize as digital entertainment began to emerge. Video games, which had their precursors before the 1980s, for example, Atari's Video Computer System and its classics "Space Invaders" and "Donkey Dong," began to change the daily lives of young people in the 80s. The appearance of the Nintendo Entertainment System and its renowned Super Mario Bros and Legend of Zelda, among others, the Game Boy in 1989, and fighting and shooting games like Mortal Kombat or Doom led to a fundamental change in the leisure activities of young people, especially boys. The next step was marked by the appearance of the Sony PlayStation and the Sega Saturn in 1994 and the Nintendo 64 in 1996. While video games were marketed across sectors, digitalization undoubtedly changed the habits of adolescent boys aged 13 through 18 first. Although they could still play on the street, many of them could now also play inside. Soon they would play games with each other remotely, too. While online games began in 1999, they were few and far between. More so than gamer meet-ups, online video games stabilized definitively in the mid-2000s.

The next great stage of digitalization is probably the most impactful and perhaps overshadowed the rest. It began with the advent of the internet, a new space of personal intercommunication which compressed interaction distances and expanded contact possibilities among people and companies. Although its purpose was essentially commercial, this later changed with the web 2.0 which helped develop any personal and social scope. The internet had been born much earlier with Arpanet, but it wasn't until the mid and late 90s that it became popular and turned into today's communicative environment. The internet's main social effect was, initially, the ability to spread information. Consequently, information became even more valuable, and Web use changed the economy, work, and every aspect of society (Castells, 2003). The possibility of acting remotely also facilitated illicit access to information, damaging or affecting it. Thus, the cybercrime that had first appeared during the 80s began to become more common. When information acquired economic value and the internet became a patrimonial place for business and entertainment, cybercrime ceased to be unusual displays of computer prowess and became regular offenses. During the early and mid-2000s and the appearance of the web 2.0, cyberspace also became a social network where people shared personal experiences, and exchanged more than just information; they essentially started to live and interact online. In this environment, the amount of social interest that is potentially affected by the behavior of motivated offenders rises significantly, and so does cybercrime. These direct changes came paired with other indirect changes to our everyday lives. The advent of the internet caused a change in the habits of those who used it. This became especially true after the appearance of social networks which constituted an essential element in addition to entertainment.

There may be a third, possibly unnoticed stage that our society currently lives in. This stage would be characterized by the definitive popularization of cyberspace, induced by the generalized usage of smartphones. But, on top of the quantitative expansion, there's a qualitative difference in comparison to the first stage of the internet. The former required a complex and limited device to access the Web remotely; the latter, thanks to the generalization of smartphones, allows users to carry cyberspace in their pockets. Opportunities increase, as cyberspace and physical space overlap, creating a hybrid world where crimes too are hybrid (Milani et al., 2022). While this stage may already be underway, it is undeniable that the Covid-19 crisis and the corresponding more or less strict lockdown regulations passed by most governments had an accelerating effect on this phenomenon. This acceleration of the digitalization process may have moved some activities to the digital environment that, even in the presence of smartphones and mobile internet, had still been considered exclusively physical activities.

This rough outline of stages of development doesn't presume discrete boundaries and hence doesn't bare the assumption that distinct factors took effect in every one of those stages. Nor does it pretend that crime evolution in each stage is categorically distinct from the others. The stages described above are an attempt at systematizing gradual processes which modify our everyday lives slowly and shift baselines subtly rather than a set of stages that abruptly change the habits and interests of people. But this structure provides a better grasp on the idea that digitalization did not produce one single, major change, but many smaller ones. Said changes can be distinct from one another since digitalization has such manifold repercussions. Perhaps the most important ones were not the direct effects, but those caused by unexpected transformations of peoples' lifestyles. It must be considered, firstly, that the digital revolution does not constitute one single change but many, secondly that it does not occur at a single point in time and is instead an evolutive process, and thirdly that the impact of such a process is multifaceted. Therefore, to comprehend the effects of digitalization as an opportunity-modifying process, types of societal changes will be grouped as follows. Firstly, digitalization effects on crime are grouped based on the type of mechanism that affects crime opportunity; secondly, on the relationship between crime types and crime opportunity types; and thirdly, on whether the change has produced more or fewer crime opportunities.

Firstly, digital technology can represent a direct or indirect change in crime opportunities. As a direct mechanism, it creates new valuable objects or goods, which may become suitable targets for potential motivated offenders. It can also decrease the value of some goods which become futile and are therefore no longer susceptible to apprehension or damage. But there might also be an indirect effect on opportunities. This occurs when technology changes the lifestyles and daily routines of aggressors and victims. The convergence of potential aggressors and suitable victims in a place of criminal opportunity can increase or decrease as a result of these changes rather than the technology itself.

This goes to show that lifestyle changes are the main modifier for criminal opportunity. Thus, if technology were introduced without resulting changes in lifestyles, criminal opportunity would be unaffected. Many of the direct changes of opportunity derived from the invention and rollout of technology are intentional (e.g., weapons, security systems). Others, however, may come about unintentionally (e.g., advances in medical technology improvements that prevent manslaughter due to better survival rates), either as predictable side effects or as genuinely unexpected phenomena.

This mixture of direct and indirect effects may cause a decrease in one crime typology (i.e., street crime) and an increase in others (e.g., cybercrime). While the connection between the two is intuitive, it is difficult to characterize this connection in detail when assuming a direct mechanism (Farrell & Birks, 2018). However, both tendencies may well be determined by a third factor that affects them differently, as explained in Fig. 4.2. Digitalization is a prime candidate for such a factor and that it affected at least two types of opportunity dynamics. On the one hand, lifestyle adjustments have been produced in different populations, at different points in time, and in different intensities throughout three decades of digitalization, bound by a common dynamic: more time spent inside and less time outside. Thus, the origination of both offenders (both in vandalism and property crime) and victims (both of violent and patrimonial crimes) decreased. However, time spent inside would generate opportunities for new and different crimes, related to activities carried out in cyberspace, now acclimated to the patrimonial and informational values that the new digital goods and objects acquired with time. This explains why the trends are not simultaneous: It is possible that the descending tendency of some outside crime types began before the rise of cybercrime. The latter could not yet have generated enough opportunities.

Comparing the relationship between these tendencies to the way pool balls clash among themselves would be reductive. This conjecture attempts to show that small changes in our daily habits can affect different opportunities simultaneously, like ripples in a fabric rather than clashing pool balls. One day comprises 24 hours, and some of them could be dedicated to activity A while disregarding activity B. It is then possible that those opportunities related to activity A increased, and those linked to B, decreased. While easy to argue, it is difficult to test.

As seen in Fig. 4.1 and further developed in Fig. 4.2, behavioral adjustments to digitalization would have taken place in different population groups, in distinct ways and at different points in time. The most prominent case will be examined in the exploration of the first specific hypothesis on the conjecture of the effects of digitalization on crime trends. Said case is related to changing habits of young

4 Crime Opportunities, Lockdowns, and Online Video Games: The Digital Leisure… 85

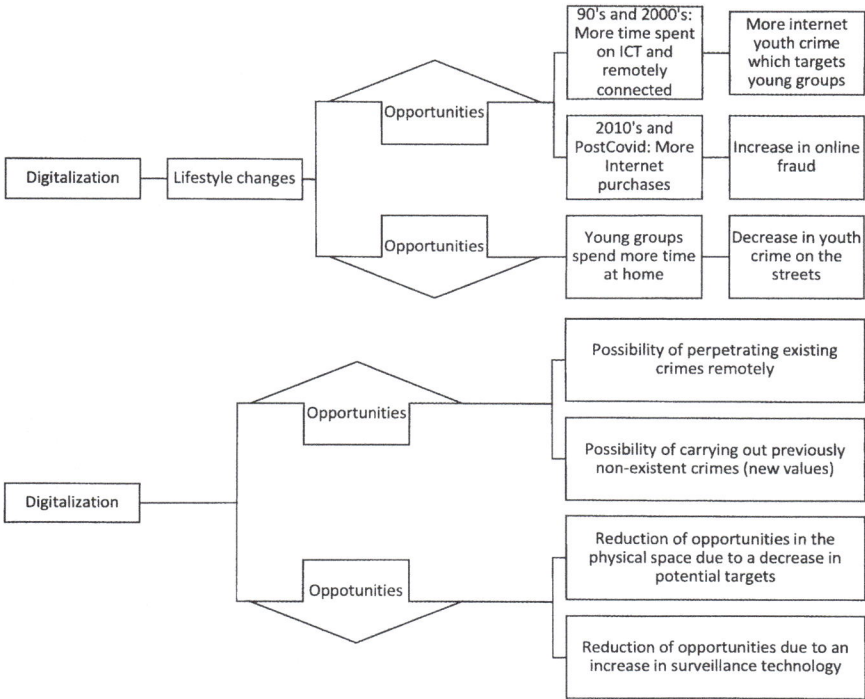

Fig. 4.1 Direct and indirect impact dynamics of digitalization on criminal opportunities

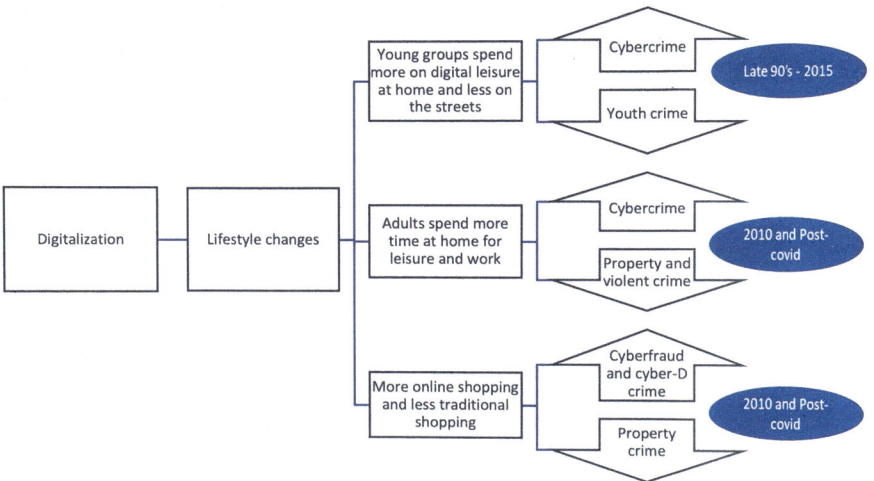

Fig. 4.2 Indirect impact dynamics of digitalization on criminal opportunities

citizens and the shift in opportunities from the street to cyberspace. According to Kerr (2005), changes to entertainment dynamics may have impacted youth crime, first with the appearance of video games and later with social networks. These may have led to a decrease in time spent on the street among young individuals and could explain the crime decline associated with them. Cybercrime, in turn, may have increased as a result of the rising number of interactions in cyberspace. This does not equate to offenders transferring criminal activity from the street to the Web. That is, criminal typologies such as cyberbullying, threats, and cyber fraud are genuine consequences of new opportunities for criminal and deviant behavior rather than substitutes for crime in physical space, as research on the evolution of such behaviors in the gaming sphere suggests.

However, lifestyle changes are not restricted to young individuals who spend more time at home as a result. This may be a general trend. But while younger audiences may be affected by this since the 90s, the phenomenon may have reached adults by the 2000s, when the internet finally became standard in homes. The growing amount of time spent at home would entail an increase in activities which would previously occur outside, such as shopping and working. Once again, a change in lifestyle such as working remotely or online shopping may have had a double effect. As workplaces and shopping malls became less busy, crime in those areas would decrease. Meanwhile, the increase in people carrying out activities of exchange of economic value online has generated more crime opportunities, and hence crime, on the internet. This tendency would have been exacerbated during the Covid-19 crisis, where reduction of mobility would affect criminal topologies, as previously argued. Differences in comparison to previous scenarios of mobility reduction are presumably continuous rather than categorical. That is, the effects of mobility on crime opportunity may be more easily detectable in the context of the Covid-19 crisis, while findings may extrapolate to general trends in mobility reduction.

All of these are related to a more direct effect of digitalization, namely, the generation and/or reduction of opportunities due to the development of information and communication technologies, as seen in Fig. X. The internet, as a new environment for communication, offers the possibility to replicate traditional crimes in cyberspace, which has also facilitated the perpetration of remote crimes. In terms of opportunity, this entails that convergence between victims and aggressors in absence of a capable guardian no longer requires physical closeness. It is now possible for the potential aggressor to converge with a suitable victim located thousands of miles away. Digitalization has also generated new, valuable objects and goods of interest for attacks. Personal data and other elements which now acquire economic value, and even cryptocurrencies, are suitable examples. These social changes translate into new opportunities and new crimes, and as long as these are properly registered, tendencies will reflect them. Lately, a significant increase in some crimes perpetrated through the internet, such as fraud, has been observed. However, even nowadays, victims do not report many cybercrimes. Sometimes official statistics fail to properly register them. Nevertheless, this does not mean they do not exist.

Technology can lead to a decrease in opportunity, and digitalization may have produced a similar direct effect in some specific situations, due to the devaluation of some objects with an economic value associated with them or the decrease in their use. Cheques and digital currency, which have been substituting regular currencies for some time now, are good examples. Moreover, technology not only affects the convergence of aggressors and victims but also the ability of guardians to avoid crimes. It is true that digitalization, through the creation of cyberspace, may have occasionally reduced the ability of guards, supervisors, and other individuals other than the victim, to avoid the perpetration of a crime, mainly in cyberspace and by formal agents, due to transnationality and anonymity (Miró-Llinares & Johnson, 2017; Miró-Llinares & Moneva, 2020). However, their ability to control physical space may have increased as a result of the implementation of digital technologies. Current evidence suggests that CCTV technology has been able to moderately reduce crime (Piza et al., 2019; Thomas et al., 2022). The future will most likely bring new technologies which will probably deepen these tendencies.

The Conjecture and Its Early Developments: On the Impact on Crime Trends Since 1990

The fragmentation of the prior points, addressing different periods of time, distinct population groups, and diverse crime types, would result in the derivation of many concrete hypotheses from the general conjecture. Specific hypotheses in regard to lifestyle changes in underage individuals and adults and their impact on the crime drop has been developed: the increase in cyberspace-perpetrated crimes which may not be well reflected in official statistics, the impact of social networks and their popularization on the growth of certain juvenile crime typologies, or theorize what Tinder and similar apps may signify for the shift in sexual offenses specifically. The goal of this chapter, in any case, is to put forth the conjecture while reinforcing its theoretical foundations and showing how plausible it is through concrete evidence. Conversely, extracting and testing every possible hypothesis in this conjecture is not the goal. However, testing the plausibility of the general conjecture requires more than a theoretical justification and requires disaggregation as was argued above.

The following section is therefore aimed at the development of specific empirical hypotheses. Furthermore, it will be discussed why these hypotheses warrant further analysis beyond the scope of this book. The focus will thus center on the two fundamental hypotheses arising from the evolving dynamics of crime tendencies due to digitalization. The first is related to indirect changes of digitalization caused by modifications in lifestyle and their impact on street crime due to the increase in time spent at home; the second is related to direct changes of digitalization produced by the appearance of a new scope of remotely perpetrated crime. The former would occur in the mid-90s and would explain, at least partially and alongside other factors, the decrease in youth crime on the streets. The latter would become manifest from the 2000s onward, with the appearance and later popularization of the internet. This tendency would have entailed an increase in crime not registered in official statistics. In the following sections, the hypotheses will be presented, briefly substantiated, and supported with research data to facilitate a more comprehensive development of our points.

The Digital Leisure Hypothesis: The Impact of the Change in the Routines of Young People Due to Digital Leisure in the So-Called "Crime Drop"

The starting point for this hypothesis is the idea that digital technology has produced deep changes in society's lifestyles. Particularly, it has meant the appearance of a new type of digital entertainment which changed how young people spend their time outside of school and their families. There is a shift from time spent on the street, in the 80s and early 90s, to homes. This change should not only have affected young individuals but also adults, with their shift being more evident in the mid-90s, and especially in the first decade of the new century. While technologies such as TV and the radio had already existed in North American homes in the 50s, a great variety of entertainment-related technologies (such as computers, gaming consoles, etc.) found their way into households in the 80s, and especially in the 90s. This change in entertainment habits would have made young individuals spend more time inside and, as a consequence, reduced crime opportunities for street crime significantly. Consideration should be noted that young individuals easily adapt to and adopt new technologies in comparison to other age groups (Morris & Venkatesh, 2000; Koenig et al., 2010). They also are one of the age groups that dedicate more time to entertainment (see Fig. 4.1) and to digital entertainment specifically (see Fig. 4.2). Therefore, the effect of digitalization on their everyday activities, especially leisure-related ones, is presumably deeper compared to other age groups (Figs. 4.3 and 4.4).

The time dedicated to these new digital activities may have been detrimental to the time destined for traditional home entertainment such as reading or watching TV. Additionally, it might have entailed a shift from street entertainment to home entertainment. In that regard, data from the American Time Use Survey (ATUS) points to a combination of these two mechanisms; it seems that the time young

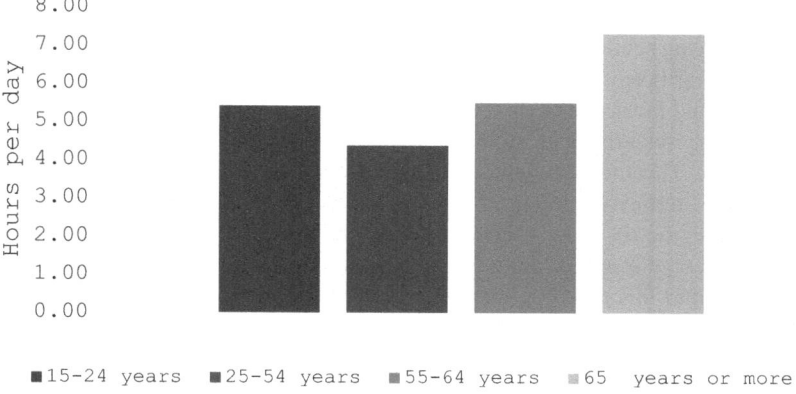

Fig. 4.3 Hours per day dedicated to leisure and sports by age group. Self-elaboration. (Data from ATUS)

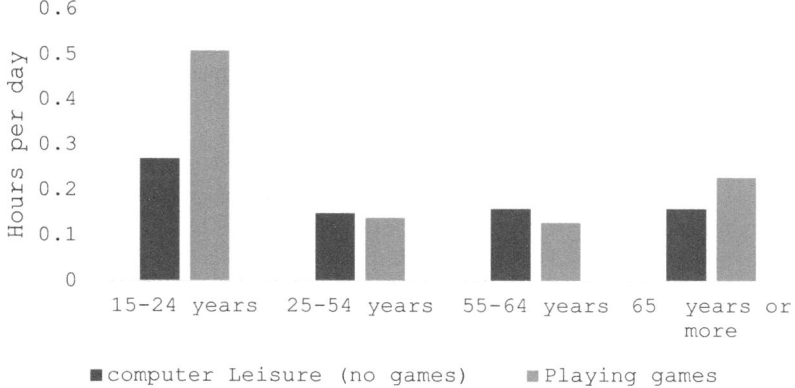

Fig. 4.4 Hours per day dedicated to PC leisure and gaming by age group. Self-elaboration. (Data from ATUS)

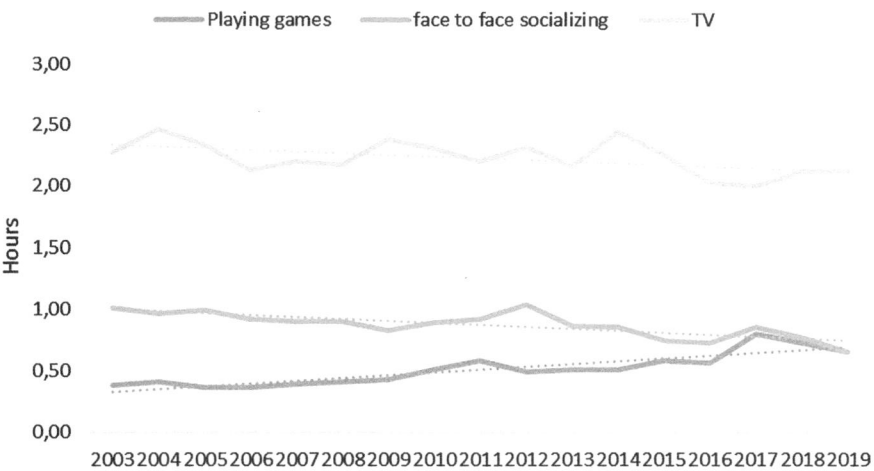

Fig. 4.5 Daily hours spent on different leisure activities (people from 14 to 25 years of age). Self-elaboration. (Data from ATUS)

individuals spend on some form of traditional home entertainment such as TV has been reduced. Similarly, the time dedicated to outside activities such as socializing (face to face) or leisure travel has also decreased. Concurrently, the time spent on digital entertainment activities[1] has increased over the years. As Fig. 4.3 shows, in 2003, young individuals spent more time socializing face to face than playing video games. By 2019, these activities occupied the same amount of time in the day of adolescents and young adults (Fig. 4.5).

---

[1] This includes video games but also includes playing traditional board games.

According to the RAT, this change in leisure activities, specifically the decrease in time spent outside versus the increase in time spent on home entertainment, would suggest a change in crime opportunities. This is explained by a decrease in convergence possibilities between offenders and victims in the physical space, by spending more time inside (both potential aggressors and potential victims) and, consequently, by rising home security levels. The first hypothesis thus states that the first change, that of time spent inside, may reduce physical victimization levels by decreasing the convergence between aggressors and targets. This factor contributes, among others, to the crime drop. Moreover, this hypothesis is consistent with previous research regarding the crime drop, as many studies suggest that the crime drop is first and foremost driven by adolescents and young adults desisting from crime (see Blumstein & Wallman, 2006; Matthews & Minton, 2018; Butt & Evans, 2014; Ganpat et al., 2020; Griffiths & Norris, 2020; Butts, 2000; Kim et al., 2016). Similarly, as stated above, the transformation of digital entertainment affected this age bracket sooner and more strongly than others.

We operationalize this by contrasting two variables for reference. This is operationalized by contrasting two variables. The first is vandalism, a crime that is strongly associated with young individuals, as measured by arrest rates by the Bureau of Justice Statistics. The second variable is the daily average of hours spent on video games by individuals of the same age bracket (between 15 and 24 years of age) since 2003 from ATUS data. Visual inspection of the progression of both variables reveals an inverse evolution. The constant increment in the time dedicated to video games appears to be selectively associated with the constant descent in vandalism arrest rates (Figs. 4.6 and 4.7).

The relationship between these two variables is explored using Spearman's correlation. A strong negative correlation is observed both for the daily hours spent on

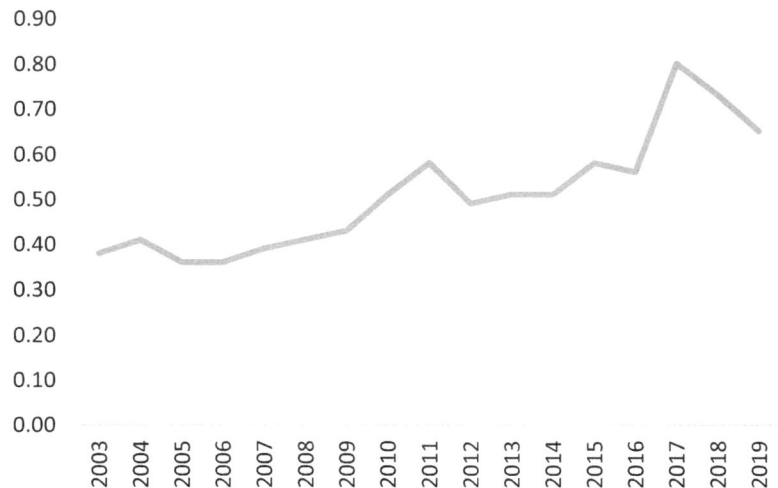

Fig. 4.6 Average time spent on gaming by young individuals. (Data from ATUS)

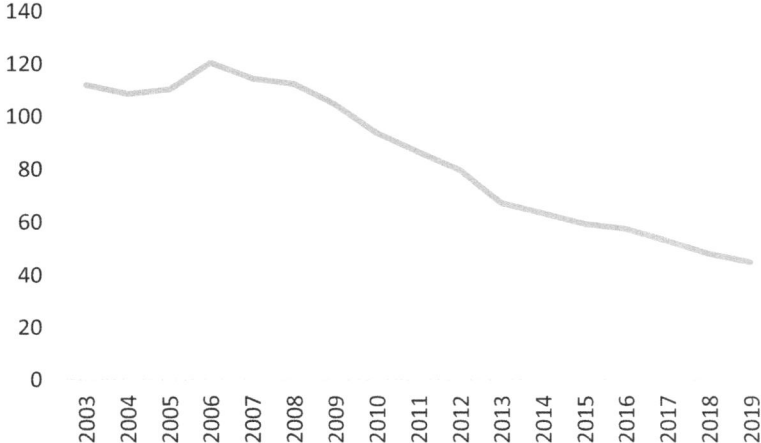

Fig. 4.7 Young arrest rate for vandalism. (Data from the Bureau of Justice Statistics)

this activity on weekdays (rho = −0.89, $p \leq 0.001$) and on weekends and holidays (rho = −0.83, $p \leq 0.001$). However, this relationship is not statistically significant among adults (older than 25). It is acknowledged that the variable measuring time spent on games is not exclusively tied to digital games. Therefore, changes in time spent on games may have evolved and increased due to factors unrelated to the proliferation of digital entertainment. If this were the case, the relationship would not provide insight into the connection between crime and digital entertainment. However, when examining the evolution of daily computer use for entertainment purposes among individuals of the same age group, excluding games, strong negative correlations are once again found with youth crime arrests related to vandalism (rho = −0.69, $p \leq 0.001$ and rho = −0.71, $p \leq 0.001$ for weekdays and holidays, respectively). This relationship remains nonsignificant in the case of adults.

According to the suggested hypothesis, digital entertainment is related to an increase in the time spent inside and, in turn, lesser rates of crimes such as vandalism. Therefore, as stated above, logic dictates that if younger age groups make broader use of technology, the decrease in arrests will be more prominent for that demographic. But since vandalism is mainly perpetrated by young individuals anyway, it is possible that the high variability in adult vandalism arrest rates is affected by other variables. To mitigate this factor, the vandalism arrest rates can be replaced with burglary arrest rates, where the representation of young individuals is not as high. The variables are, again, negatively associated and Spearman's correlations are highly significant. The negative association is stronger for young individuals (rho = −0.85, $p \leq 0.001$) than for adults (rho = −0.67, $p \leq 0.001$). These results are, once again, consistent with the suggested hypothesis and point at a potential inverse relationship between digital entertainment and arrest rates. Additionally, the relationship is stronger in young groups, who consume more electronic entertainment.

Although previous analyses suggest a negative association between time spent on digital entertainment and youth crime arrest, the lack of relative data available prior to 2003 impedes the detection of a possible time synchrony between digital entertainment and the crime drop in the early days of digitalization. In order to analyze a wider time period, further data sources and an analytical strategy inspired by Kerr's study on techno-leisure and crime rates could be used. This approach was applied using a construct called digitalization rate. Three variables comprise the construct, namely, penetration rates of personal computers, the internet, and mobile phones in homes in the United States, according to World Data Bank data. This allowed us to widen the analysis from 1994 (when personal computers and consoles existed, but before browsers, the popularization of the internet, and the advent of mobile technology) to 2016, when these technologies had completely penetrated American homes. The study employed data relative to different crime arrest rates registered by the Bureau of Justice Statistics as the independent variable. Linear regression was conducted to analyze the relationship between digitalization rates, general arrest rates, and different crimes in young individuals and adults. The most relevant results revealed that the arrest rate model for every crime is statistically significant and explains a notable percentage of data variance. Additionally, the negative association of digitalization rates with crime arrest rates is stronger in the case of younger individuals ($R^2 = 0.769$, $\beta = -706.16$, $p \leq 0.001$) compared to adults ($R^2 = 0.915$, $\beta = -473.07$, $p \leq 0.001$).

This result points in the direction of the hypothesis, namely, that technology and its impact on everyday activities seem to be related to the crime drop, especially among younger age groups. Nevertheless, the change in those activities may not have had the same impact on every crime type. Thus, vandalism arrest rates, which are associated with younger perpetrators, and burglary were analyzed separately as a subset of general crime rates. Prior research has found more consistent associations for violence against property than for violent crime. Significant results were obtained for vandalism, which explain big portions of the variance for both younger groups and adults. Again, digitalization rate shows a stronger association in young adults ($R^2 = 0.761$, $\beta = -22.74$, $p \leq 0.001$) than in adults ($R^2 = 0.742$, $\beta = -3.43$, $p \leq 0.001$). Similarly, the model is also significant in regard to burglary, and digitalization rate again exhibits a stronger association in young individuals ($R^2 = 0.824$, $\beta = -27.49$, $p \leq 0.001$) than in adults ($R^2 = 0.567$, $\beta = -6.11$, $p \leq 0.001$).

The macro-level adoption of technologies in American households, which relates directly to the time spent inside, seems to inversely affect arrest rates, serving as a proxy for real crime evolution. This effect seems to be more prominent among young individuals who use technology the most and enjoy the leisure activities connected to it. Therefore, researchers should not discard the impact of technology on crime drop. Rather, it seems to be a relevant factor, which is supported at least by the US American data and should thus be taken into account in research on the crime drop. However, the linear regression models construe the relationship between variables linearly, as their name suggests. Similarly, it must be considered that simple single predictor models, which do not theoretically control for confounding variables, may be a naive approximation. As a counterpoint, one could argue that the

Table 4.1 Linear regression models for arrest rate and digitalization rate

	All crimes		Vandalism		Burglary	
	R^2	β	R^2	β	R^2	β
Youth	0.769	−706.16***	0.761	−22.74***	0.824	−27.49***
Adults	0.915	−473.07***	0.742	−3.43***	0.567	−6.11***

*** $p < 0.001$

variances of the dependent variables are sufficiently well accounted for by the models to be rejected or ignored in advance. However, it should be recalled that the goal of this project is to sustain a general conjecture with preliminary results rather than exploring single hypotheses in excessive detail (Table 4.1).

Despite the preliminary character of this research, the digital leisure hypothesis is an increasingly promising explanation for the descent in some forms of youth crime. Evidently, more research is needed. Additionally, the conjecture will not be complete without considering the larger amount of time young groups have been spending in the new space of criminal opportunity that is cyberspace, which began its development in the year 2000.

Building the New Digital Opportunities Hypothesis: About the Hidden But Real Impact on Trends in the Emergence of New Media to Perpetrate Internet Crime

In the previous section, this chapter suggested that the reduction in leisure time spent on the streets, as opposed to an increase in leisure activities at home, would suppose a change in crime opportunities as a result of a decrease in convergence possibilities between offenders and targets in the physical environment. However, a fundamental shift in everyday activities was purposefully obviated, which this segment will address. Digitalization has created new virtual spaces and, in turn, the possibility of convergence therein. An increase in time spent inside, as a consequence of an increase in time spent in cyberspace, logically supposes an increment in the chances of convergence within this new space. Moreover, new everyday activities have appeared along with new interests in cyberspace, generating new crime opportunities. Therefore, digital technology has spawned new crime opportunities linked to both new (e.g., informatic systems, data) and classic interests (e.g., patrimony, personal interests) with exponential speed. This phenomenon began in the 90s but caught a second wave with the arrival of the internet in households. It furthermore exacerbated the scope and modalities of crime, as well as the number of victims, despite police statistics failing to reflect this.

The change in lifestyles as a result of the appearance of new technologies influences people in two different ways, which should be understood as two faces of the same coin. Firstly, there would be a reduction in crime opportunities, since, as stated above, there is an increase in the time spent at home. Secondly, said time increase, namely, spent in cyberspace, may, in turn, provoke an increment in crime opportunities in this environment, especially when new activities and interests appear. The best example of such a shift is probably online shopping. According to Federal Reserve Economic Data, online shopping constituted 1% of the total sales of the retail sector at the beginning of the twenty-first century. Meanwhile, current figures indicate that 18% of all retail sales are carried out online. This has two important consequences for the evolution of criminal tendencies. Firstly, the appearance of cyber-delinquency such as fraudulent sales in online stores is an obvious direct consequence. Secondly, an example of an indirect consequence might be the typical amount of cash carried by potential victims in the physical space. When business is mainly carried out online, general habits may shift toward not carrying cash, reducing the opportunity for crime in the physical space, especially in combination with the popularization of credit cards, bank transfers, or even payment via smartphone, as mentioned earlier in this chapter.

A second hypothesis emerges from the connection between the digitalization process and crime tendencies: The appearance of new technologies and their fast popularization may have created new digital spaces for criminal opportunity, which may increase digital crime. The observation of the economic losses (adjusted to inflation) caused by crimes reported to the IC3 (see Fig. 4.3) and the evolution of

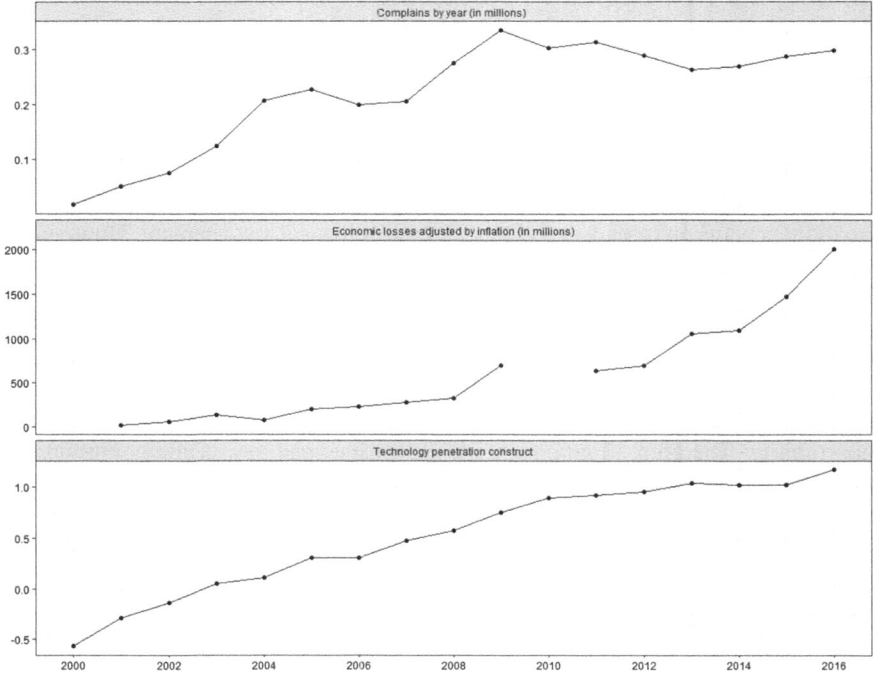

Fig. 4.8 Report and loss number evolution known by IC3 compared with the digitalization construct evolution

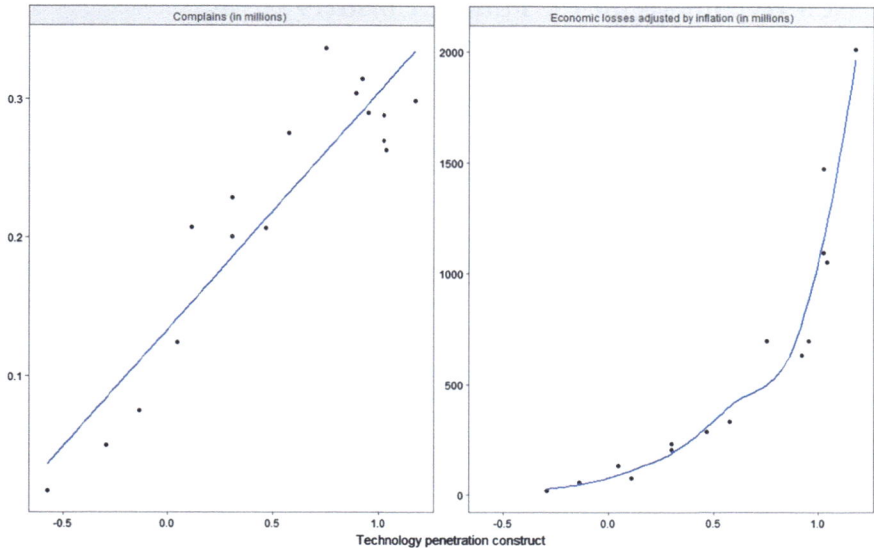

Fig. 4.9 Relation between technology penetration and cybercrime

reported crimes reveals an increase in both reports and losses, similarly to the digitalization rate. Visual inspection of the connection between digitalization rates and the two aforementioned variables suggests a linear association in the case of reports but an exponential one in the case of economic losses. A linear regression model of digitalization rates and the number of reports confirms this strong association ($R^2 = 0.856$, $\beta = 0.17$, $p \leq 0.001$). Including an exponent in the regression model verifies the apparently strong link between economic losses and the penetration of technology in North American homes ($R^2 = 0.951$, $\beta = -2.72$, $p \leq 0.001$). The model explains 95% of the variance of the dependent variable (Fig. 4.8).

Despite some data gaps, three increasing tendencies in reports per year can be identified (which seem to decrease or stably fluctuate from 2009 on), economic losses (adjusted to inflation), and in technological penetration (Fig. 4.9).

In previous analyses, these models only included a single predictor. They are, however, consistent with the conjecture that the increase in everyday online activities as a result of digitalization caused an increase in cyber-victimization levels, as measured by the number of victims and registered losses. The effect of digitalization on opportunity shifts cannot be ignored, particularly in the case of certain criminal typologies.

As shown in the previous section, crime rates in the physical space have been decreasing since the 90s as a result of the increase in time spent inside, which reduces crime opportunities. Conversely, cyber-victimization rates increase as a consequence of everyday activities carried out in cyberspace. Physical analyses do not support a shift from physical delinquency to cyber-delinquency. They simply show a decrease in physical crime and an increase in cyber-delinquency.

A New Hypothesis for the Future: Covid-19 Crisis, the Acceleration of Digitalization and Future Crime Trends

As the previous section has shown, the digital transformation has a double effect on crime trends. Firstly, it reduces crime opportunities in the physical space due to digital habits and their impact on mobility. Secondly, criminal opportunity increases in cyberspace. While this development started slowly in the early 90s, it was drastically accelerated in March 2020 and since, because the Covid-19 pandemic has forced citizens to suspend physical interaction as a means to prevent infections. The establishment of restrictive measures in most countries provoked a direct and immediate impact on mobility which lasted for some time but also changed habits of interaction and everyday activities in the long term. Increases in remote work and online shopping, which seem to have remained at much higher rates than those prior to the pandemic crisis, are indicative of this. These changes have had an effect on cybercrime, and now see that the shifts in physical and online delinquency are returning to pre-pandemic conditions, as prevention measures are slowly taken back and old living habits are reclaimed. However, changes to many everyday activities will stay, and those users who did not buy online and started doing so during the quarantine will likely retain this new habit. The results put forth by Buil-Gil, Zeng y Kemp (2021) similarly suggest that many traditional crime types decreased after the lockdown but subsequently snapped back to pre-pandemic levels. On the other hand, their results suggest that cyber-dependent fraud and delinquency increased and stayed higher than before the pandemic. Therefore, one can assume that the Covid-19 crisis will be another point of change, similar to the advent of the internet and the arrival of social networks. While this change is not linked to the appearance of new technology, it translates to an increase in its use by many segments of the population.

Future contributions will have to assess the impact of new societal habits derived from social and leisure technologies on delinquency. Moreover, the impact of each technological shift on different criminal typologies must be specified. Digitalization will never cease to advance and it is uncertain whether human mobility will end up increasing or decreasing. Much closer attention will have to be paid to a phenomenon that may have affected the evolution of crime rates to a far greater extent than everyone could imagine.

References

Abrams, D. S. (2021). Covid and crime: An early empirical look. *Journal of Public Economics, 194*, 104344. https://doi.org/10.1016/j.jpubeco.2020.104344

Aebi, M. F., & Linde, A. (2010). Is there a crime drop in Western Europe? *European Journal on Criminal Policy and Research, 16*(4), 251–277.

Agrawal, S., Kirchmaier, T., & Villa-Llera, C. (2022). *Covid-19 and local crime rates in England and Wales-two years into the pandemic* (No. cepcovid-19-027). Centre for Economic Performance, LSE.

Blumstein, A., & Wallman, J. (2006). The crime drop and beyond. *Annual Review of Law and Social Science, 2*, 125–146.
Braudel, F. (1958, December). Histoire et sciences sociales: la longue durée. *Annales. Histoire, Sciences Sociales* 13, 4, 725-753). Cambridge University Press.
Buil-Gil, D., & Zeng, Y. (2021). Meeting you was a fake: Investigating the increase in romance fraud during COVID-19. *Journal of Financial Crime, 29*(2), 460–475. https://doi.org/10.1108/jfc-02-2021-0042
Buil-Gil, D., Miró-Llinares, F., Moneva, A., Kemp, S., & Díaz-Castaño, N. (2020). Cybercrime and shifts in opportunities during COVID-19: A preliminary analysis in the UK. *European Societies, 23*(sup1). https://doi.org/10.1080/14616696.2020.1804973
Buil-Gil, D., Zeng, Y., & Kemp, S. (2021). *Offline crime bounces back to pre-covid levels, cyber stays high: Interrupted time-series analysis in Northern Ireland*. https://doi.org/10.21428/cb6ab371.64bc853e
Butts, J. A. (2000). *Youth crime drop*. Report.
Butts, J., & Evans, D. (2014). The second American crime drop. In *Juvenile justice sourcebook* (Vol. 61).
Castells, P. (2003). La web semántica. In *Sistemas interactivos y colaborativos en la web* (pp. 195–212).
Cheung, L., & Gunby, P. (2021). Crime and mobility during the COVID-19 lockdown: A preliminary empirical exploration. *New Zealand Economic Papers, 56*(1), 106–113. https://doi.org/10.1080/00779954.2020.1870535
Cromwell, P., Dunham, R., Akers, R., & Lanza-Kaduce, L. (1995). Routine activities and social control in the aftermath of a natural catastrophe. *European Journal on Criminal Policy and Research, 3*(3), 56–69. https://doi.org/10.1007/bf02242928
Díaz, C., Fossati, S., & Trajtenberg, N. (2021). Stay at home if you can: Covid-19 stay-at-home guidelines and local crime. *SSRN Electronic Journal*. https://doi.org/10.2139/ssrn.3932628
Farrell, G., & Birks, D. (2018). Did cybercrime cause the crime drop? *Crime Science, 7*(1). https://doi.org/10.1186/s40163-018-0082-8
Ganpat, S. M., Garius, L., Tseloni, A., & Tilley, N. (2020). Violence and the crime drop. *European Journal of Criminology, 19*(44), 767–790. https://doi.org/10.1177/1477370820913456
Gerell, M., Kardell, J., & Kindgren, J. (2020). Minor covid-19 association with crime in Sweden. *Crime Science, 9*(1). https://doi.org/10.1186/s40163-020-00128-3
Griffiths, G., & Norris, G. (2020). Explaining the crime drop: Contributions to declining crime rates from youth cohorts since 2005. *Crime, Law and Social Change, 73*(1), 25–53.
Halford, E., Dixon, A., Farrell, G., Malleson, N., & Tilley, N. (2020). *Crime and coronavirus: Social distancing, lockdown and the mobility elasticity of crime*. https://doi.org/10.31235/osf.io/4qzca
Jenkins, P., & Phillips, B. (2008). Battered women, catastrophe, and the context of safety after Hurricane Katrina. *NWSA Journal, 20*(3), 49–68.
Johnson, S., & Nikolovska, M. (2022). *The effect of covid-19 restrictions on routine activities and online crime*. https://doi.org/10.31235/osf.io/ze49b
Kemp, S., Buil-Gil, D., Moneva, A., Miró-Llinares, F., & Díaz-Castaño, N. (2021). *Empty streets, busy internet. A time series analysis of cybercrime and fraud trends during COVID-19*. https://doi.org/10.31235/osf.io/38wfy
Kerr, J. D. (2005). *Crime rates and the technological transformation of leisure: A routine activities approach*. University of Kentucky.
Khweiled, R., Jazzar, M., & Eleyan, D. (2021). Cybercrimes during covid -19 pandemic. *International Journal of Information Engineering and Electronic Business, 13*(2), 1–10. https://doi.org/10.5815/ijieeb.2021.02.01
Kim, M. T., & Leung, F. (2020). COVID-19 pandemic and crime trends in NSW. *Australasian Policing, 12*(3).
Kim, J., Bushway, S., & Tsao, H. S. (2016). Identifying classes of explanations for crime drop: Period and cohort effects for New York State. *Journal of Quantitative Criminology, 32*(3), 357–375.

Kirchmaier, T., & Villa-Llera, C. (2020). Covid-19 and changing crime trends in England and Wales. *Centre for Economic Performance*, (013).

Koenig-Lewis, N., Palmer, A., & Moll, A. (2010). Predicting young consumers' take up of Mobile Banking Services. *International Journal of Bank Marketing, 28*(5), 410–432. https://doi.org/10.1108/02652321011064917

Kotkin, J. (2002). *The new geography: how the digital revolution is reshaping the American landscape.* Random House.

Lallie, H. S., Shepherd, L. A., Nurse, J. R. C., Erola, A., Epiphaniou, G., Maple, C., & Bellekens, X. (2021). Cyber security in the age of covid-19: A timeline and analysis of cyber-crime and cyber-attacks during the pandemic. *Computers & Security, 105*, 102248. https://doi.org/10.1016/j.cose.2021.102248

Langton, S., Farrell, G., & Dixon, A. (2020). *Six months in: Pandemic crime trends in England and Wales.* https://doi.org/10.31235/osf.io/t7ne8

LeBeau, J. L. (2002). The impact of a hurricane on routine activities and on calls for police service: Charlotte, North Carolina, and Hurricane Hugo. *Crime Prevention and Community Safety, 4*(1), 53–64. https://doi.org/10.1057/palgrave.cpcs.8140114

López, E., & Rosenfeld, R. (2021). Crime, quarantine, and the U.S. coronavirus pandemic. *Criminology & Public Policy, 20*(3), 401–422. https://doi.org/10.1111/1745-9133.12557

Matthews, B., & Minton, J. (2018). Rethinking one of criminology's 'brute facts': The age–crime curve and the crime drop in Scotland. *European journal of criminology, 15*(3), 296–320.

McCarthy, M., Homel, J., Ogilvie, J., & Allard, T. (2021). Initial impacts of COVID-19 on youth offending: An exploration of differences across communities. *Journal of Criminology, 54*(3), 323–343. https://doi.org/10.1177/00048658211005816

Milani, R., Molnar, L., Caneppele, S., & Aebi, M. F. (2022). Convergence of traditional and online property crime victimization in a city with little offline crime. *Victims & Offenders*, 1–18. https://doi.org/10.1080/15564886.2022.2036659

Miró-Llinares, F. (2021). Crimen, cibercrimen y covid-19: Desplazamiento (acelerado) de Oportunidades y Adaptación situacional de Ciberdelitos. *IDP. Revista De Internet Derecho y Política*, (32). https://doi.org/10.7238/idp.v0i32.373815

Miró-Llinares, F., & Johnson, S. (2017). Cybercrime and place: Applying environmental criminology to crimes in cyberspace.

Miró-Llinares, F., & Moneva, A. (2019). What about cyberspace (and cybercrime alongside it)? A reply to Farrell and Birks "did cybercrime cause the crime drop?" *Crime Science, 8*(1). https://doi.org/10.1186/s40163-019-0107-y

Miró-Llinares, F., & Moneva, A. (2020). Environmental criminology and cybercrime: Shifting focus from the wine to the bottles. In *The Palgrave handbook of international cybercrime and cyberdeviance* (pp. 491–511). Palgrave Macmillan.

Morris, M. G., & Venkatesh, V. (2000). Age differences in technology adoption decisions: Implications for a changing work force. *Personnel Psychology, 53*(2), 375–403. https://doi.org/10.1111/j.1744-6570.2000.tb00206.x

Nivette, A. E., Zahnow, R., Aguilar, R., Ahven, A., Amram, S., Ariel, B., et al. (2021). A global analysis of the impact of COVID-19 stay-at-home restrictions on crime. *Nature Human Behaviour, 5*(7), 868–877.

Piza, E. L., Welsh, B. C., Farrington, D. P., & Thomas, A. L. (2019). CCTV surveillance for crime prevention: A 40-year systematic review with meta-analysis. *Criminology & Public Policy, 18*(1), 135–159.

Reid, J. A., & Baglivio, M. T. (2022). Covid-19's impact on crime and delinquency. *Crime & Delinquency, 68*(8), 1127–1136. https://doi.org/10.1177/00111287221084295

Riddell, J. R., Piquero, A. R., Kaukinen, C., Bishopp, S. A., Piquero, N. L., Narvey, C. S., & Iesue, L. (2021). Re-opening Dallas: A short-term evaluation of COVID-19 regulations and crime. *Crime & Delinquency, 68*(8), 1137–1160. https://doi.org/10.1177/00111287211054718

Stickle, B., & Felson, M. (2020). Crime rates in a pandemic: The largest criminological experiment in history. *American Journal of Criminal Justice, 45*(4), 525–536. https://doi.org/10.1007/s12103-020-09546-0

Thomas, A. L., Piza, E. L., Welsh, B. C., & Farrington, D. P. (2022). The internationalisation of cctv surveillance: Effects on crime and implications for emerging technologies. *International Journal of Comparative and Applied Criminal Justice, 46*(1), 81–102.

Verano, S. P., Schafer, J. A., Cancino, J. M., Decker, S. H., & Greene, J. R. (2010). A tale of three cities: Crime and displacement after Hurricane Katrina. *Journal of Criminal Justice, 38*(1), 42–50. https://doi.org/10.1016/j.jcrimjus.2009.11.006

Open Access This chapter is licensed under the terms of the Creative Commons Attribution 4.0 International License (http://creativecommons.org/licenses/by/4.0/), which permits use, sharing, adaptation, distribution and reproduction in any medium or format, as long as you give appropriate credit to the original author(s) and the source, provide a link to the Creative Commons license and indicate if changes were made.

The images or other third party material in this chapter are included in the chapter's Creative Commons license, unless indicated otherwise in a credit line to the material. If material is not included in the chapter's Creative Commons license and your intended use is not permitted by statutory regulation or exceeds the permitted use, you will need to obtain permission directly from the copyright holder.

Chapter 5
Observing, Measuring, and Researching Cybercrime: A Scoping Review of Systematic Reviews Since 2010s

Stefano Caneppele

Introduction

While the rest of the chapters of this book discuss the role of digitalization in decrypting crime trends and propose new hypotheses for the future, this chapter inquires what criminologists and non-criminologists have done concerning the definition of cybercrime and its research. In particular, the chapter provides a scoping review of scientific contributions in published systematic reviews between January 1, 2011 and December 31, 2021. This chapter aims at providing an overview on what have been done for studying (and thus empirically measuring) cybercrime by scholars in recent years. In detail, the chapter covers the data that have been used and the analytical methods that have been applied to the study of cybercrime. The majority of empirical contributions addressing cybercrime have found publication in journals spanning various disciplines. This can be attributed to the widespread interest, sparked by the emergence of cybercrime, within the scientific community. Notably, the involvement of criminologists in the study of cybercrime has been relatively limited. Nevertheless, it should not be neglected that nowadays an increasing number of criminologists have been studying cybercrime and its manifestations, and they have been confronted with the issues of its definition and its measurement. These issues are recurrent, especially in social sciences when facing emerging phenomena. For criminologists, who also rely on positivists approaches when studying crime and deviance, criminal law definitions have not been very helpful, since the pace of digital revolution and innovation are overwhelming the functioning of national criminal justice systems. In fact, our contemporary society lives the

S. Caneppele (✉)
School of Criminal Sciences, Faculty of Law, Criminal Sciences and Public Administration, University of Lausanne, Lausanne, Switzerland
e-mail: stefano.caneppele@unil.ch

information age. According to Merriam-Webster (nd), this term refers to "a time in which information has become a commodity that is quickly and widely disseminated and easily available especially through the use of computer technology." This century is the first in which a tremendous quantity of information may be stored in digital archives and retrieved when necessary. The number of digital devices, online platforms, and social media grew exponentially and thus the number of data generated through them. New disciplines such as Data Science have been established to assist this growth. In this sparkling world of data, information on deviance and crime still struggles on their traditional constraints made of dark numbers and external/internal validities issues. Neither the most recent forms of crime, mostly rebranded with the suffix cyber-, have been exempted by these burdens. To the contrary, being the newcomers, cybercrime is even more exposed to these constraints while there is an increasing demand for knowledge about its nature, characteristics, and modus operandi. In this chapter, concepts from Merton's theory (Merton, 1968) are borrowed to argue that the information age has increased the gap between the society expectations about the volume, granularity, and punctuality of information about cybercrime and their means to measure it. Coping with such strain generates different ways of responding, following Merton's theory: conformity, innovation, ritualism, retreatism, and rebellion. Under the conformity response, data on cybercrime should be progressively incorporated into the official crime statistics systems acknowledging the need to provide more and more accurate figures on its volumes, at least for a selected type of cybercrimes. Within the innovation responses, institutions experiment new method to gather data on cybercrime. Under the ritualism response, some argue that national crime statistics should be used as a valid source of cybercrime, since the dark number always existed for many crimes. With the retreatism response, since cybercrime is nowadays impossible to measure accurately, one should avoid providing figures, waiting for better times and/or tools. Within the rebellion response, the challenges of measuring cybercrime should not be accepted, since more and more crime will become hybridized, leaving the cyber-debate a trace of the past. All these different responses may be partially right, since from one side there is a need for policymakers and the public opinion to have figures and trends that could shape measures but, from the other side as well, the current public debate around figures of cybercrimes sometimes is echoing the counting clouds' reproach that a Dutch colleague did some years ago about the exercise of measuring organized crime in Europe (van Duyne, 2006). Thus, to start from the beginning, one should inquire about the epistemological posture of measuring (cyber)crime(s) and their trends.

On the Challenges in Measuring (Cyber)crime(s) and Their Trends

Measuring crime and deviance remains a primary aim of criminological research. Epistemologically, the concept of measurement is strictly related to the empirical observation. What can be measured is what can be observed. Observations align with what is considered compliant with the operational definition of the phenomenon being measured. This positivist approach, since the XIX century, supported the development of empirical methods to gather and collect data with the aim of understanding how human societies work.

At the same time, the positivist view also proved useful in a period of consolidation of the nation states that needed statistics primarily on the number of prisoners in prisons and convicted persons to measure the functioning of the justice apparatus. As far as crime is concerned, statistics on the numbers of offenses committed, at least as far as continental Europe is concerned, began to be compiled after the adoption of penal codes that allowed classification by offenses. This approach, although very rational from the point of view of administrative operation, was at first methodologically limited for the study of deviance and crime. First of all, lacking adequate techniques and methodologies for the collection of primary data, studies relied on secondary data such as official administrative statistics. These statistics, in turn, have at least two main methodological limitations. The first refers to the quality of the data. The researcher has to rely on the data provided without being able to control how the data was produced. The second limitation concerns classification. Criminal statistics primarily respond to an administrative demand and are therefore constructed according to the facts of the criminal codes of the country of reference. These cases not only vary from country to country, creating a problem of comparison (Aebi et al., 2014), but also group together behaviors that have different criminological characteristics, making it impossible for the researcher to break down the crime according to its multiple dimensions. For example, the broad category of homicides can include those committed by (organized) crime and those committed within the family, which have very different causes and modus operandi. It is evident that over the last 50 years police statistics have improved in their ability to provide a valid indicator of the state of apparent crime and in providing information on the evolution of crime in its various forms. However, the British experience, which is certainly to be counted among the most advanced and comprehensive in providing a measure of crime trends over time, also cautions us on the importance of quality control and data entry procedures (see UK Statistics Authority, 2014). It is precisely from the recognition of the limitations of official statistics that victimization surveys were born, which in some countries have established themselves as a necessary complement for measuring crime and its evolution.

When talking about cybercrime, this labored path of producing statistics that can provide a reliable time evolution of the situation in a region or country is largely called into question. At present, the positivist view of being able to provide a line of evolution of crime seems to have stopped in the offline world. From another perspective, the arrival of online crime can be useful to question the meaning of crime statistics and their use. Currently, these statistics are mainly used to answer two questions: (1) What is, usually over a 1-year period, the prevalence of crime in a given country and in its organizational subunits; (2) how crime in a given country and in its organizational subunits evolve, usually over a multiyear period.

The spatial component has therefore always been a fundamental key to police statistics. The fact that crime insisted on a defined territory implied that it mainly affected the communities of individuals settled on that territory. From a security policy point of view, this implied that when faced with a territory with high crime intensity, the authorities would allocate more resources to reduce the frequency and/or severity of crime and to observe whether the measures taken had an impact on crime levels over time. Again, crime levels depended at least in part on specific environmental characteristics of the territory itself (e.g., being a tourist location, having a population density) that require local actions on which public actors can have a direct influence.

However, this approach to the use of crime statistics remains, for much of cybercrime, meaningless. In the online world, there are various cyber places that, parallel to the physical world, may present criminogenic environmental elements that are independent of the physical environment and beyond the control of local and often national decision-makers. Without necessarily referring to the dark Web and its illegal market, consider, for instance, the case of sites accessible on the clear Web that promise to sell match-fixing news in order to make money from sports betting (Moneva & Caneppele, 2020). As with appropriative crimes, other types of online crimes (e.g., Web defacement or DNS attacks) are entirely carried out in cyberspace, disengaging the perpetrator/victim relationship from the dimension of the territoriality of the act. Indeed, if the consequences on the victims may have a known territorial impact, the same cannot be said of the perpetrator.

It is precisely this territorial disconnect that makes it more difficult for victims to identify the police as an effective interlocutor, influencing the victims' propensity to report crimes. To this should be added that for many cybercrimes, technology has made it possible to multiply criminal productivity by increasing the volume of attempted and consumed crimes. All this contributes to increasing the gap between the demand for security and the public resources available to respond to it. While the gap between supply and demand for protection from online crime seems to have widened considerably, it should be emphasized that this is not a recent phenomenon (Ratcliffe, 2008). This widening gap began to be observed as early as the 1960s and the various Western societies have adapted to these problems mainly by outsourcing some security services considered less of a priority (airport security, shopping malls, etc.) to private entities, creating a market for private security services, developing new security technologies accessible to the general public (e.g. armored doors, video surveillance systems), and/or developing insurance mechanisms for damage reduction by transferring the burden to private citizens. Likewise, a similar process could be observed in a more recent period with regard to the dimension of protection from cybercrime with the implementation of a market for services and the adoption of soft- and hard-law systems to (self-)regulate the market itself. This insistence of a plurality of actors in cybersecurity policies has generated at the same time a variety of statistics, more or less business oriented, produced by private commercial actors whose cyclicality and scientific validity often remains variable. The common trait that characterizes the majority of these statistics is the reference to a customer-based and not country-based dimension and the orientation toward specific forms of cybercrime, especially with respect to what are considered to be threats to the cybersecurity world. While this proliferation of reports and statistics is in line with the logic of quantifying the severity and frequency of a phenomenon, it also makes it possible to emphasize how often, especially on the part of policymakers, there is an underestimation of the complexity and variety of conducts that are simply summarized under the umbrella term "cybercrime." In fact, in order to measure a phenomenon, a compulsory step is to operationalize it as accurately as possible, in order to allow comparability over time and between different studies. The next section discusses the concept of cybercrime and its definitions.

To Be, or Not to Be (Cybercrime), That Is the Question

As emphasized in the previous paragraph, the first methodological issue to be addressed when measuring a phenomenon is its operationalization. In this case, it is interesting to note how the rapidity of technological evolution has affected the operationalization of the concept of cybercrime. In the beginning, crimes committed with the use of computers were simply referred to as computer crimes to highlight the central role of the device in the commission of the crime. Most crimes were related to fraud that could be committed by manipulating or stealing data, although there was already a widespread practice of hacking into telephone companies' telematics systems to avoid paying the costs of long-distance calls, which were still very expensive in the 1980s and 1990s. While the first viruses and malware had already made their appearance in the 1980s, it was with the spread of the internet first on landlines and then on cell phones that a quantitative and qualitative mutation of online crime took place. This change of pace is also mirrored in the definition of these crimes, where the term computer crimes is gradually being replaced by the term cybercrimes to emphasize that the computer component of the crime is not limited only to the physical medium on which the software is installed but refers to a broader ecosystem that goes by the name of cyberspace. Some empirical evidence about the evolution of the terminologies comes from McGuire (2019) who compared the number of occurrences in the literature when describing the phenomena of cybercrime in the period 1995–2000 and 2001–2018. Although the difference in the time spans, it is evident how the term cybercrime has gained its relevance compared to the term computer crime, while other terms such e-crime or internet crime are becoming more popular as well. Alongside the terminological evolution in the academy, a doctrinal debate has also developed. The main academic debate that has been going on for many years can be summed up in the debate on the validity of the saying "old wine in new bottles." Indeed, researchers are divided on whether the advent of cybercrime represents a new challenge for criminology, even from a theoretical point of view. There are those who support the applicability of classical criminological theories and those who instead emphasize the peculiarities of cybercrime and thus the need to develop new theories capable of explaining the emerging phenomenon. In fact, the arguments in favor of one or the other perspective depend—in the field of criminology—on the type of cybercrime under consideration. This brings us back to the starting point of all research: the operationalization of the cybercrime concept. In the 1980s and 1990s, a broad perspective, derived from the term computer crime, was favored, in which emphasis was placed on the mere presence of a device to refer to this new category of crime. This was an understandable approach at the time, since there was no cyber-universe with a wealth of places for interaction. Today, being connected is a constancy. Technological evolution has enabled the creation of virtual spaces of convergence in which individuals interact by moving behavior from the remote to the online (e.g., cyberbullying, hate speech) with the aggravating factor that hyper-connectedness allows reaching a potentially larger number of users. In addition, the development of the digital infrastructure has created criminal opportunities for the commission of crimes that directly attack the infrastructure and its terminals on which the very functioning of the cyber world and its platforms depends. This dichotomy echoes one of the most frequently used typologies in the literature, which distinguishes between cyber-enabled and cyber-dependent crime. This classification includes, on the one hand, those crimes that already existed before, one usually takes the example of fraud, but which have taken advantage of the Web to increase their effectiveness and spread. On the other hand, cyber-dependent crimes are all those crimes that could not exist if the digital infrastructure did not exist: for instance, malware that exploits system vulnerabilities or DNS attacks that aim to render a website inactive.

The evolution of the debate around cybercrime categorizations is summarized in the contribution by Phillips et al. (2022) who identify the most widely used taxonomies in the literature and their evolution by proposing a new classification with the aim of also incorporating new trends that include, for instance, the exploitation of artificial intelligence in the commission of crimes. The new model incorporates the contribution of previous classifications (see, e.g., Gordon & Ford, 2006; McGuire, 2019; Tsakalidis & Vergidis, 2019; D. Wall, 2007; D. S. Wall, 2001, 2015) and combines them in order to provide a broader view of the relationship between information technology and criminal conduct. The taxonomy starts from the consideration that theoretical reflection on the classification of the various behaviors that may fall under the category "cybercrime" is still immature but that it is necessary to advance the debate out of scientific needs and to improve prevention and law enforcement policies.

The fluidity of the cybercrime concept poses problems not only from the point of view of research validity but also from the point of view of official statistics. If from a scientific point of view, it becomes difficult to compare studies using different operational definitions; from the point of view of official statistics, the challenge to capture the full dimension of the cyber contribution to criminal conduct is even bigger. Already with Caneppele and Aebi (2019), he pointed out the difficulties for statistical systems in dealing with relatively recent phenomena such as cybercrime. The challenges are manifold, often starting with the identification of the crime as cyber, the classification of the conduct, and the way it is accounted for. Setting up a statistical system requires time and measures to ensure a consistent collection methodology over the years, to guarantee monitoring and comparability of the observed trends. In this sense, the efforts observed in official criminal justice statistics are as follows. Firstly, there is the legalistic approach that incorporates the new cybercrimes into the national criminal codes, including the reported phenomenon by referring to the relevant criminal code article in full. This is often the case for conduct classified as cyber-dependent, that is, conduct integrating attacks and/or tampering with computer systems. These offenses were mostly introduced after 2004 following the transposition of the Budapest Convention of the Council of Europe on cybercrime. The data collected for these offenses have little significance for measuring the extent of the phenomenon and should rather be read as the responsiveness of national legal systems to cybercrime conducts. Secondly, there is a more minimalist approach that aims to extend the cyber component to all types of recorded crime by asking the data operators to flag a box if the crime is cyber-related. This solution is probably the easiest to implement in systems that require the involvement of a very large number of actors in the imputation of data, as is the case in the United States, for instance. The concluding acts of the Committee on the Reform of American Statistical Systems (National Academies of Sciences, Engineering, and Medicine, 2018) suggested this strategy to start observing, in a more systematic manner, the contribution of the technological component in the commission of criminal conduct. It is evident that, apart from the advantages, this strategy also has limitations in providing detailed information. In this context, it appears more advantageous to collect data concerning the phenomenon of cybercrime without aspiring to encompass universal cyber behaviors. Instead, the focus should be directed toward a more delimited selection of conducts. From this perspective, the use of victimization surveys was considered a useful response and it should be considered a third approach. Well known, for instance, is the England and Wales crime victimization survey (CSEW) that, for several years now, has been collecting the experiences of British citizens who declare themselves victims of computer misuse and cyber-related fraud incidents. Despite the limitations and biases concerning the nature and online crimes observed by victims, the CSEW surveys provide a first impression of the weight of the cyber component on the observed criminal conduct, which is stably around one-third of the total crime. A fourth, more ambitious approach has more recently been developed to offer a broader categorization of what is called digital crime. It is the one proposed in Switzerland by the collaboration between the Federal Statistical Office (FSO) and the Swiss cantonal police forces. Under the term digital crime, the FSO defines those "offences committed on telecommunication networks, in particular the Internet" (Federal Statistical Office, 2023). The classification is operated by the cantonal police on the basis of crime modus operandi according to five major areas: economic cybercrime (24 modus operandi), cyber sexual crimes (4 modus operandi), cyber damage to reputation and unfair practices (3 modus operandi), darknet (1 modus operandi), other (1 modus operandi). This experiment, which started in the late 2010s, led to the publication of the first Swiss police crime statistics with an indication of the digital component. Although the data need consolidation and the classification is subject to change, it is interesting to note that even in the Swiss context, at least on the basis of the latest available data (2021), the incidence of digital crime accounts for approximately one-third of the total crime.

It is beyond the scope of this chapter to present a more detailed survey of the challenges of measuring cybercrime in official statistics, be it police statistics or victimization surveys. For a more detailed discussion, refer to the contributions that were produced with other colleagues at a conference organized by the Council of Europe on these very issues (Aebi et al., 2022). In general, it can be concluded that to date there is still a certain fluidity in the definition of cybercrime. This fluidity is the result of the fact that the digital world is expanding rapidly. National statistical systems cannot advance at the same pace and adapt themselves by following different strategies depending on the available resources and the characteristics of the relevant statistical system. The next section investigates how academic research has studied cybercrime in the recent decade (2011–2021), which theories it has used, and what knowledge it has produced with respect to which types of cybercrime.

Scoping the Empirical Research on Cybercrime

To investigate the empirical criminological research on cybercrime, a search on Google Scholar was conducted to identify the systematic reviews or meta-analysis published in journal articles between January 1, 2011 and December 31, 2021[1] which mentioned the keyword cybercrime.[2] The search allowed to trace 37 systematic reviews/meta meta-analysis, most of them (28) have been conducted between 2017 and 2021.[3] All the relevant manuscript cited in their reference sections were reviewed and all mentioned journal articles (even those published before 2011) which a) reported a quantitative study that b) formulated hypotheses on c) any kind of cybercrime and its characteristics (offenders, victims, and modus operandi) d) concerning criminological theories, offenders, and victims were included. Those articles focusing on research techniques, measures effectiveness, and cybersecurity have been excluded. The initial screening allowed to identify 436 articles, which have been reduced to 344 after a quick abstract scrutiny and then to 74 following the abovementioned requirements. Obviously, this approach has been followed in order to reduce the number of articles that could fit in the empirical testing of cybercrime, while selecting only articles mentioned in systematic reviews could serve as an indicator of the impact of the article in the scientific community. Of course, this research does not presume to be exhaustive, since the search was only done in English, but some general trends may be investigated. Table 5.1 summarizes the variables that were collected during the review of the articles included in the analysis.

---

[1] The author extends sincere appreciation to Ms. Sandra Ribeiro for her valuable assistance in retrieving manuscripts from the systematic reviews and preparing a database for analysis.
[2] The exact search query was cybercrime AND ("systematic review" OR "meta-analysis").
[3] We found, respectively, no relevant systematic reviews on cybercrime in 2011, 1 in 2012, 0 in 2013, 1 in 2014, 3 in 2015, 2 in 2016, 4 both in 2017 and 2017, 5 both in 2019 and 2020, and 10 in 2021.

Table 5.1 List of variables identified

Variable	Description
Title	Title of the manuscript
Journal	Journal of the manuscript
Author(s) of publication	Name(s) of author(s)
Year of publication	Year of publication of the study
Country	Country where the study was conducted
Keywords	Keywords of the study
Phenomenon	Phenomenon studied
Purpose	Goal of the study
Research question/hypothesis	Questions and/or hypothesis of the study
Data collection period	Start month-year (and end month-year) of data collection
Type of study	Type of study identified 1. Longitudinal study / 2. Experimental study / 3. Empirical study
Type of data	Type of data collected by the study (1. Primary data (e.g., self-reported crime survey, victimization survey) / 2. Secondary data (e.g., official statistics))
Data collection method	Data collection method used in the study. 1. Survey / 2. Experimental condition / 3. Other
Participants	Number and type of participants included in the study 1. Legal person / 2. Natural person
Type of analysis	Type of analyses performed as part of the study
Answer to research question/hypothesis[a]	Answer to the research question and/or hypothesis; research question and/or hypothesis substantiated by the study 1. Yes / 2. No / 3. Partly

[a]Sometimes research questions have been formulated vaguely. Therefore, it is not possible to answer to the questions

Our data should be helpful to provide some answer to four broader questions: 1) Which cybercrime has been more investigated by criminologists according to the Google Scholar search? 2) Which criminological and non-criminological theories have been more often the subject of empirical testing? 3) Which types of data and analytical method have been used? 4) Which are the most relevant findings of these studies.

Before answering these questions, it is relevant to note that quantitative studies on different types of cybercrime have not found a place in the most important generalist criminological journals. This can probably be explained by the fact that, as with crime statistics, journals take time to adapt their editorial line. This has therefore favored (1) the creation of new journals specializing in aspects of cybercrime that have intercepted this demand for publications that had no place in traditional journals and (2) the spread of criminological studies in more interdisciplinary journals. However, it is important to point out that for some online crimes, especially those involving interpersonal violence (e.g., sexual crimes), the interest in online abuse has resulted in traditional journals opening to these new research perspectives. Finally, it should be mentioned that most of the selected studies originated from research carried out in Anglo-Saxon countries, particularly in the United States (approximately 50%). The presence of research concentrated in continental Europe accounts for about one-tenth of the total sample taken into consideration. It should be emphasized that this gap can be attributed to at least two factors: On the one hand, it is the product of a delay in the study of cybercrime in Europe, which has only been investigated systematically in the last decade, and on the other hand, it is due to the fact that European academia is less interested in topics related to interpersonal violence (bullying), sexual abuse, and the consumption of child pornography, topics that have historically been much more analyzed in Anglo-Saxon countries. These issues and their digital transposition were among the first to be studied and researched.

Which Cybercrimes Have Been More Investigated?

In the previous paragraphs, said it was already stated that the concept of cybercrime embraces several criminal behaviors. The review confirms that, from an academic point of view, discussing about cybercrime is pointless without disentangling its several dimensions. Figure 5.1 shows that the highest number of studies on the

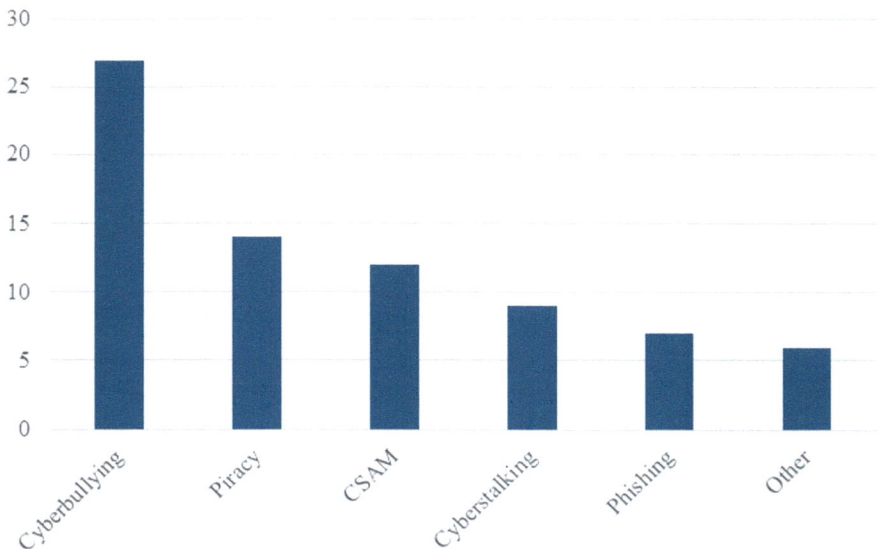

Fig. 5.1 Frequency distribution of cybercrime types identified in the review ($N = 75$) a (in the case of an article addressing both cyberbullying and cyberstalking collectively, each was counted both under cyberbullying and cyberstalking categories)

online criminal behaviors focused on cyberbullying (27 cases), followed by online piracy (14),[4] child sexual abuse material (12), cyberstalking (8), and phishing (7).

It is noteworthy that criminal behavior which is considered often falls within the category of traditional crimes imported into the digital sphere. In most instances, the digital development is consistently observed to be interconnected with behavior in the physical realm. Based on this observation, it is reasonable to presume that researchers who have previously focused on this topic have oriented their studies toward examining the impact of digital innovation on such behaviors. This holds true for most crimes of interpersonal violence; however, the discourse differs for issues such as online piracy and phishing, which are relatively recent phenomena that have garnered the attention of researchers seeking to understand the factors that contribute to an inclination toward online piracy, as well as the susceptibility to phishing.

Likewise of the debate around the broader concept of cybercrime, even for these specific categories of online crime, scholars highlight the lack of shared operational definitions of the phenomenon, raising issues of comparability. For example, in the case of cyberbullying, a plurality of terms (cyberbullying, electronic bullying, cyber harassment, e-bullying) have been used, which more recently seem to be consolidating toward a single term (cyberbullying). However, the problem of the plurality of operationalizations of the concept remains. Price et al. (2013) points out that there are different techniques for measuring cyberbullying that can explain, at least in part, the discrepancies in prevalence rates. Indeed, some define cyberbullying as an extension in the digital space of bullying and use the three characteristics identified by Olweus (1993) as an aggressive behavior that is (1) intentional, (2) repetitive, and (3) based on an interpersonal relationship characterized by a systematic imbalance of power and domination (Alsawalqa, 2021). Other authors take only the first two points of the definition of Olweus, adding the online component and replacing the last component with the intention of causing harm or distress to others (see, e.g., Li, 2010; Zalaquett & Chatters, 2014). Similarly, to the existing debate on the concept of cybercrime, it is interesting to note that the same type of debate also occurs within specific subcategories of online crimes, such as bullying and cyberbullying (Kubiszewski et al., 2015). In this area, researchers have divided between supporters of the continuity of behaviors and supporters of the novelty of behaviors and their consequences. In particular, the latter have emphasized how the different nature depends (Bauman & Pero, 2011) from the anonymity of the cyberbully, the limitless potential audience, the shift in power dynamics, and the lack of limitations on time and location.

Finally, it should be noted that a minority of the studies taken into account consisted of experimental studies that mainly focused on phishing victimization experiences ($N = 7$).

---

[4] Online (or digital) piracy is defined as "The illegal copying and/or downloading copyrighted software, music, video, or other material such as MP3s, Hollywood movies, and digital audiobooks" (Cronan & Al-Rafee, 2008, p. 528).

Which Criminological and Non-criminological Theories Have Been More Tested?

The foundation of criminology lays on corroborating hypotheses from theories that explain deviance and crime. When it comes to cybercrime, the manuscripts analyzed suggested that, in the last decade, the effort was mainly devoted in exploring and detecting correlations among personal characteristics and the cybercrime (from the offender and the victim's perspective) and its eventual distinction between online and offline crime characteristics. As already mentioned, most of the reviews targeted traditional forms of offline crime that moved to the online environment, such as cyberbullying and cyberstalking. However, it is important to observe that the topic of cybercrime have been analyzed from several disciplines each one bringing their theoretical constructs in understanding the phenomena. From the criminological perspective, it should be noted that the most recurrent theories used were the routine activity theory (RAT) (Cohen & Felson, 1979) and social control theory (Gottfredson & Hirschi, 1990). The routine activity theory, in its initial formulation, posited that the crime was the result of the convergence in time and space of three components: a motivated offender, a suitable target, and the lack of a capable guardian. The theory is a development of a lifestyle theory (Hindelang et al., 1978) in the sense that it focuses most of its attention in explaining victimization and the targets' characteristics (e.g., through the acronyms VIVA (valuable, inertia, visibility, accessibility) or CRAVED (concealable, removable, available, valuable, enjoyable, disposable)). The perspective of analyzing offenders' characteristics remained largely unexplored. In the last 40 years, the theory evolved toward more advanced conceptualization (Eck & Madensen, 2015), adding further elements to the initial construct (e.g., handler, super controllers). Nevertheless, the theory was conceived to explain predatory crimes in physical spaces. Despite some early criticisms (Yar, 2005) about its adaptability to the new cyberenvironment, the RAT was largely used and tested by many scholars with divergent results. A systematic review on 24 papers published between 2015 and 2021[5] about the use of RAT on cybercrime (Ahmad & Thurasamy, 2022) suggests that divergency may also depend from approximate operationalization of the RAT theoretical constructs. Indeed, there is a need to further operationalize RAT's components since "exposure, target attractiveness, and guardianship constructs need to be formulated and differentiated across cybercrime" (Ahmad & Thurasamy, 2022, p. 424).

While the routine activity theory provided most of its valuable contribution in explaining victimization patterns, the social control theory was definitely conceived to explain why a person may become an offender. The theory was designed to be applicable to any form of criminal or deviant behaviors (Pratt & Turanovic, 2014). It posits around the concept of self-control. According to the theory, individuals with no or low self-control tend to engage in crime more often than other people.

---

[5] The review was not considered in our study because it was not in our predetermined interval (between January 1, 2011 and December 31, 2021).

The low self-control individuals are more prone to crime since they cannot control their impulse for excitement and immediate gratification while they overlook the long-term consequences of their action (e.g., conviction). Indeed, this theory explains why having considered the same context and the same set of opportunities, some individuals offend and others not. Low self-control acts as a trigger to deviance and criminal conducts although itself cannot fully explain crime propensity (see, e.g., Cochran et al., 1998). Coming to its applicability to the online environment, the social control theory has been used in the field of cyber-enabled crime such as digital piracy (Aleassa et al., 2011), cyberstalking (Fissel et al., 2021; Reyns et al., 2018), and child pornography (Clevenger et al., 2016). Beyond the criminological theories, two other cognitive theories have been repeatedly used in the reviews considered: the theory of reasoned action (TRA; Ajzen & Fishbein, 1980) and its extension the theory of planned behavior (TPB; Ajzen, 1985). The conceptual pillars of these theories are behavioral beliefs and attitude, normative beliefs and subjective norms, control beliefs and perceived behavioral control, and intentions (La Caille, 2013). Behavioral beliefs encompass the convictions that individuals associate with a specific behavior (e.g., "If I engage in studying, I anticipate improving my knowledge, achieving good grades, and expanding my job opportunities"). These convictions concurrently shape the individual's attitude toward the anticipated outcomes of the behavior (e.g., "Engaging in studying and achieving good grades is a positive endeavor"). The strength of this favorable attitude correlates with the intensity of the intention to act in accordance with these beliefs.

Normative beliefs involve the perceived expectations of significant individuals in one's life regarding the behaviors of the individual in question (e.g., "My friends believe that I should prioritize studying"). These beliefs induce social pressure, fostering compliance (e.g., "I feel compelled to study to align with my friends' expectations"). Control beliefs encompass convictions concerning the factors that may facilitate or impede a specific behavior (e.g., "I possess sufficient time to dedicate to studying during the week and possess the necessary skills to excel academically"). These convictions subsequently contribute to shaping the perception of behavioral control, denoting the confidence in one's ability to execute a particular behavior (e.g., "I am confident in my ability to study effectively for my exams"). Intentions, in this context, signify the willingness to engage in a specific behavior based on the aforementioned beliefs.

Both these theories (theory of reasoned action and theory of planned behavior) assume that the best predictor to engage in a certain behavior is the intention to act. Intentions are determined by attitudes and subjective norms. Then, as explained by La Caille (2013, p. 2231), "the more positively a person regards a certain behavior or action and the more they perceive the behavior as being important to their friends, family, or society, the more likely they are to form intentions to engage in the behavior." The theory of reasoned action later evolved into the theory of planned behavior, emphasizing the significance of volitional control not only in forming intentions but also in executing the behavior guided by those intentions. These psychological theories recall and combine similar concepts from other classical criminological theories, such as the theory of differential association (Sutherland, 1940), the social learning theory (Akers, 1973), social bond theory (Hirschi, 1969), and the rational choice theory (Cornish & Clarke, 1986), with regard to the intentions to act. The utilization of theories beyond criminological frameworks to explore cybercrime is indicative of the extensive array of disciplines that have cultivated an interest in this emerging research domain.

Which Types of Data and Analytical Method Have Been Used?

Another aspect worth highlighting concerns the data used to analyze cybercrime. The preferred data tool was the survey, used as the sole or primary data collection tool for 51 out of 74 of the studies considered. The survey targeted a highly variable number of respondents, ranging from 30 to 6379 (Table 5.1). Most of the studies relied on small sample with less than 250 ($n = 18$) or between 251 and 500 participants ($n = 12$). All the studies focused on individuals, primarily adolescents or college students ($n = 34$), with a sample size of a few hundred cases. Other contributions relied on the public of adults ($n = 10$) recruited also through Amazon Mechanical Turk and Web survey while a minority targeted offender ($n = 4$), employees ($n = 1$), or clients ($n = 1$). The preference for young and student population is explainable, by the prevalence of the themes addressed (e.g., cyberbullying, online piracy), by the greater accessibility of this population through primary data collection, and by the propensity of young populations to provide honest answer to surveys. Nevertheless, the review highlights a proliferation of studies with limited samples that raise doubts about external validity. The problem of generalizability of the results is recurrent and the consolidation of knowledge in this field appears fragile. However, these are recurrent problems and typical in emerging areas of study, which tend to decrease over time as studies increase in quantity. It should be noted that ten manuscripts used secondary data collected through survey. Even for secondary data, the privileged population were student and adolescent although, in this case, the average sample is higher compared to primary data collected through primary survey (2739.72 vs. 716.75) suggesting more robust results in terms of external validity. Nevertheless, the use of secondary data is exposed to the risk of internal validity since usually the survey is not designed on purpose and researcher have no control over the operationalization of the variables (Table 5.2).

Table 5.2 Survey as primary data. Participants by size[a]

Size range	N (count)	Min	Max	Average	Standard deviation
0–250	18	33	245	162.88	63.40
251–500	12	264	482	341.00	78.04
501–750	6	503	714	598.83	63.15
751–1000	6	759	974	844.50	82.27
> 1000	9	1007	6379	2319.66	1647.89
Total	51	33	6379	716.75	1040.10

[a]The remaining studies used secondary data from surveys, official statistics or legal databases (17), or collected primary data for other research designs (6) (e.g., experimental conditions)

In the domain of analytical methods, a substantial portion of the examined studies opted for descriptive or fundamental approaches to inferential statistics, utilizing techniques such as linear regression and ANOVA. Others combined descriptive statistics with more sophisticated techniques. Eventually, a minority of the scrutinized manuscripts embraced more sophisticated methods to validate theoretical frameworks, such as structural equation modelling (SEM).

In the former approach, the primary objective was to delineate the sample's characteristics, provide an estimate of the prevalence of the targeted cybercrime behavior, and discern existing differences between groups, particularly victims and non-victims of a specific cybercrime. This methodology found application in a comprehensive study investigating cyberstalking on a specific social media platform in Germany, where a sizable population sample ($N = 6379$) was analyzed (Dreßing et al., 2014). Nevertheless, a descriptive approach was adopted even in smaller sample such as Li (2010) who explored, through a sample of 269 Canadian students, their beliefs and behaviors associated with cyberbullying. The intermediate approach was used, for example, by Kaakinet et al. (2018) who first provided some descriptive data of cyber-victimization and then they used hierarchical regression models to predict the association between cybercrime victimization and subjective well-being. Similarly, Bauman and Pero (2011) combined descriptive statistics about bullying and cyberbullying prevalence among deaf and non-deaf students but using multiple imputation (MI) technique to handle missing data.

In the latter approach, statistical methodologies were employed to substantiate the constructs of theories. A noteworthy example is the study conducted by Cronan and Al-Rafee (2008), which utilized structural equation modelling to assess the theory of planned behavior within the context of digital piracy. This was the first among other studies that later adopted the structural equation modelling to corroborate the theory of planned behavior to piracy (Aleassa et al., 2011; Liao et al., 2010; Yoon, 2011). In another contribution (Wright & Marett, 2010), SEM was used to test which of the six factors in their theoretical model influenced the likelihood that an individual become a victim of a phishing email.[6] Additionally, Holfeld and Leadbeater (2015) used confirmatory factor analysis—the first step of structural equation modelling—to establish whether the proposed single constructs of cyberbullying behaviors and of victimization experiences worked. Finally, Schoeps et al. (2020) used SEM to outline which were the risk factors for being a victim of online grooming in a sample of 1200 adolescent from 16 schools in the Basque Country (Spain).

---

[6] In their study, Wright and Marett concluded that "experience and training appear to be the most effective tools for guarding against phishing" (2010, p. 289). In particular, higher level of computer self-efficacy, Web experience and, security knowledge together with a suspicion of humanity reduced the likelihood of victimization.

What Are the Findings of Criminological and Non-criminological Research?

Empirical studies aim at providing additional findings to existing knowledge about phenomena. Scientific articles typically advance existing knowledge through a systematic process of trial and error, formulating hypotheses for validation. However, in cases where the knowledge base within a domain is underdeveloped, and clear hypotheses grounded in theories or prior research are lacking, exploratory studies may pose one or more research questions for investigation. Within the sample of 74 articles, 62 were found to present hypotheses for validation (Table 5.3). Notably, when considering various types of cybercrimes, a substantial proportion of manuscripts on cyberbullying and cyberstalking (almost one-third of studies) solely presented research questions. In contrast, exceptions were observed for digital piracy, child sexual abuse material (CSAM), and phishing, where the absence of hypotheses was uncommon. While the percentage of hypotheses not corroborated falls within the expected range (ranging from 0% to 25.3% for piracy), this information underscores the issue of selection bias in published manuscripts. It becomes evident that journals may exhibit a preference for publishing research producing findings and corroborating hypotheses, potentially neglecting papers that seemingly fail to corroborate initial hypotheses. Furthermore, insights into distinct approaches in research paper composition are noteworthy. Academics within computer studies and security, particularly those publishing on piracy and phishing, tended to formulate a higher number of hypotheses per paper (averaging 7.1 for piracy and 7.3 for phishing). This stands in contrast to scholars from other disciplines (in particular human and social sciences), where cyberbullying, CSAM, and cyberstalking studies

Table 5.3 Number of manuscripts per cybercrime topic, number of studies with hypotheses, total number of hypotheses, average number of hypotheses per study, and number and percentage of non-corroborated hypothesis

Phenomenon	N of articles	N of studies with hypotheses	N of hypotheses	Average n of hypotheses per study	N of non-corroborated hypotheses	% of hypotheses not corroborated
Cyberbullying	27	18	45	2.5	4	9.0%
Piracy	14	14	99	7.1	25	25.0%
CSAM	12	11	23	2.1	5	22.0%
Cyberstalking	9	6	17	2.8	2	12.0%
Phishing	7	6	44	7.3	7	16.0%
Other studies	6	5	7	1.4	0	0.0%
Total	75	60	235	3.9	43	18.3%

[a]Fifteen studies exclusively formulated research questions (e.g., "What is the prevalence and co-occurrence of online and face-to-face victimization?" "What happens after students are cyberbullied?")
[b]In the case of an article addressing both cyberbullying and cyberstalking collectively, each was counted both under cyberbullying and cyberstalking categories for data accuracy

tended to feature a more limited number of hypotheses (2.4, 2.1, and 2.8, respectively). In the following paragraphs, an overview—for the five categories of cybercrime investigated (CSAM, cyberbullying, cyberstalking, phishing, and piracy)—of the corroborated and non-corroborated hypotheses is provided.

Child sexual abuse materials (CSAM). With regard to the 11 (out of 12) studies that corroborated hypotheses, 18 out of 23 hypotheses got corroborated totally or partially. Among these, Aslan and Edelmann (2014) found that internet CSAM offenders not convicted for contact offenses[7] have different characteristics compared to sex contact offenders and from dual offenders (both internet and contact offenses). Their findings supported a previous study by Elliott et al. (2009) which found that internet and contact offenders had different clinically observable deficits. Also, Aslan and Edelmann (2014) found that internet offenders are less likely to have had previous convictions which corroborated previous findings from Eke et al. (2011).

The investigation by Long et al. (2013) focused on the differences between CSAM offenders with and without contact, finding that dual and noncontact IIOC (Indecent Images of Children) offenders can be differentiated by the quantity and quality of the images they possess. Dual offenders tend to have fewer but more explicit sexual content images, often matching the age and gender of their contact sexual offense victims. Additionally, dual offenders are more likely to engage in grooming behaviors, produce CSAM, and possess higher-level Sexual Assault Paraphilia (SAP) content compared to their noncontact counterparts. This pattern suggests dual offenders take deliberate actions to possess IIOC that reflect their sexual fantasies and are more criminogenic with increased access to children. The existence of different categories of sex offenders was also corroborated by other studies (e.g., Seto et al., 2006; Seto et al., 2012). Those charged with child pornography offenses display heightened sexual arousal to children during testing, distinguishing them from counterparts without a history suggestive of pedophilia or those referred for sexological evaluations. Further distinctions emerge when comparing different offender categories (Seto et al., 2012). From a criminal justice perspective, another study showed that explanations provided by offenders are also influenced by the timing of questioning, reflecting nuances in the interview purpose (evidence vs. clinical) and interview style (Seto et al., 2010). For instance, the police sample of offenders, interviewed postarrest but preconviction, gave fewer explanations and were less likely to report pornography addiction compared to the clinical sample. Another study on a Canadian sample suggested that judges consistently deliver more stringent sentences to contact offenders compared to noncontact offenders (Jung & Stein, 2012). Five hypotheses across the examined studies remain uncorroborated. Contrary to expectations, findings suggest that internet offenders are not significantly more likely to have suffered from substance use disorders compared to contact offenders (Aslan & Edelmann, 2014). Furthermore, the hypothesis asserting

---

[7] Internet offenders are convicted for possessing indecent images while contact offenders are convicted for having committed an actual and direct abuse of children. Those offenders who have committed both previous offenses are called dual offenders or internet-contact offenders.

that dual offenders possess a higher quantity of child sexual abuse material (CSAM) than internet offenders did not find support (Long et al., 2013). Similarly, the hypothesis positing a correlation between contact with mental health services and internet offenses does not find substantial support (Aslan & Edelmann, 2014). Another uncorroborated hypothesis challenged the assumption that individuals viewing more extreme images online are also more prone to committing contact offenses (Long et al., 2013). Finally, the expectation that consumers of illegal child pornography exhibit below-average IQ, poor professional status, and distinctive social relationship patterns was not corroborated (Frei et al., 2005).

Cyberbullying. With regard to the 20 (out of 27) studies that corroborated hypotheses, 40 out of 45 hypotheses got corroborated totally or partially. The empirical evidence derived from the examined studies substantiates several hypotheses. Firstly, a confirmed relationship exists between the perpetration of cyberbullying and victimization in online environments (Alsawalqa, 2021). Moreover, a discernible likelihood was established that students subjected to traditional bullying experiences at school are prone to encountering cyberbullying incidents (Beran & Li, 2007). Additionally, the study found that students contending with both cyberbullying and traditional school-based bullying exhibit comparable challenges in functioning at school, equating those students who solely face cyberbullying (Beran & Li, 2007). Another cluster of corroborated hypotheses underscores the association between cyber-victimization and a longitudinal escalation in depressive symptoms, with the intervening factor of rumination (Feinstein et al., 2014). Gender-specific patterns emerged, delineating the amplification of bullying effects for males in externalizing behaviors and for females in manifestations involving internalizing deviance. Furthermore, the studies confirmed the heightened involvement of students with attention-deficit/hyperactivity disorder (ADHD) in cyberbullying activities (Heiman et al., 2015). The research findings also lend support to the mediating functions of cyberbullying and cybertrolling in explicating the associations between psychopathy, sadism, and problematic social media use (PSMU) (Kircaburun et al., 2018). Lastly, substantiated hypotheses encompass the overlap in engagement between traditional and cyberbullying, distinctive psychosocial attributes characterizing students involved in cyberbullying, and familial factors indirectly predicting bullying dynamics through individual risk and protective elements (Low & Espelage, 2013). Only a minority of hypotheses did not corroborate. Firstly, no statistically significant differences in the mean cyber-victimization on the Adolescent Cyber-Victimization Scale (CYBVICS) were observed among students of different nationalities. Additionally, there was no significant interaction detected between the sex and nationality of students of East and Southeast Asian descent on the CYBVICS (Alsawalqa, 2021). Furthermore, the application of the routine activity theory (RAT) to explain the odds of experiencing cyberbullying by girls did not yield overall support (Navarro & Jasinski, 2013). Moreover, the assumption that being a victim of traditional bullying is related to victimization by electronic bullies was not substantiated. Lastly, the expectation that youngs who cyberbullied others were more likely to be bullied than those who did not cyberbully others did not find empirical backing in the examined studies (Seiler & Navarro, 2014).

Cyberstalking. With regard to the 6 (out of 9) studies that corroborated hypotheses, 15 out of 17 hypotheses got corroborated totally or partially. Among these, gender-based perceptions are delineated, highlighting the tendency for male perpetrators to be perceived as more dangerous and engaged in illegal cyberstalking compared to their female counterparts, who are often viewed as nonthreatening (Ahlgrim & Terrance, 2021). Similarly, male victims have reduced credibility and less sympathetic portrayals than their female counterparts. The context of cyberstalking, whether perpetrated by a stranger or an ex-intimate, influences perceived threat levels. Furthermore, gender differences emerge, with women more likely to recognize and attribute behaviors to cyberstalking, displaying lower victim-blaming tendencies compared to men (Ahlgrim & Terrance, 2021). Moving beyond perceptions, the perpetration of cyberstalking is linked to individual traits, with low self-control and moral disengagement identified as predictors of engagement in such behaviors (Fissel et al., 2021). Additionally, the associations of Machiavellianism and narcissism with problematic social media use (PSMU) are elucidated through cyberbullying and cybertrolling (Kircaburun et al., 2018). Moreover, students with low self-control are more prone to engage in cyberstalking, and participation in piracy or sexting increases the likelihood of online stalking behaviors (Reyns, 2019). The victimization aspect of cyberstalking is also explored, emphasizing the direct and positive relationship with low self-control, opportunity, and control imbalances (Reyns et al., 2018). Contrary to the expectations, the hypotheses that cyberstalkers would exhibit a higher likelihood of having multiple victims and making explicit threats due to the ease and anonymity of online interactions did not receive support in the studies reviewed (Cavezza & McEwan, 2014).

Phishing. With regard to the 6 (out of 7) studies that corroborated hypotheses, 37 out of 44 hypotheses got corroborated totally or partially. Most of the studies investigated the characteristics that made people more vulnerable to phishing. Numerous hypotheses related to anti-phishing measures, victimization factors, and individual characteristics have been corroborated across various studies. Exposure to anti-phishing information, whether in different amounts or types, consistently resulted in significant differences in trust evaluations among participants (Baker et al., 2008). Fear-based phishing attacks were more likely to result in victimization than reward-based attacks, and the presence of leakage cues decreased the likelihood of phishing victimization. Increased knowledge and experience with email and phishing-specific emails led to increased attention and elaboration of phishing messages (Harrison et al., 2016). Various factors, including argument quality, source credibility, genre conformity, and time pressure, were found to influence the likelihood of victimization (Luo et al., 2013). Additionally, factors such as attention to email elements, level of involvement, email load, domain-specific knowledge (Vishwanath et al., 2011), and commitment types (normative, continuance, affective) (Workman, 2008) were identified as significant contributors to susceptibility to phishing attacks. Moreover, perceptions of cyber self-efficacy,[8] Web experience, security awareness,

---

[8] In another study considered (Vishwanath et al., 2011), a positive relationship between computer self-efficacy and elaboration of the phishing email was not found.

and suspicion of humanity were associated with a decreased likelihood of being deceived by phishing emails (Wright & Marett, 2010).

Other hypotheses across the examined studies remain uncorroborated. Contrary to expectations, the presence of leakage cues did not lead to increased attention and elaboration of phishing messages (Harrison et al., 2016) and email load did not show a negative relationship with the level of attention given to specific email elements (Vishwanath et al., 2011). Furthermore, people who are more reactant did not succumb to social engineering more frequently than those who are more resistant (Workman, 2008). Disposition to trust did not increase the likelihood of being deceived by a phishing email, and higher perceived risk did not decrease the likelihood of deception (Wright & Marett, 2010).

Piracy. With regard to the 14 (out of 14) studies that corroborated hypotheses, 74 out of 99 hypotheses got corroborated totally or partially. It should be noted that some of the studies investigated specific types of piracy targeting music (Plowman & Goode, 2009), software (Aleassa et al., 2011), and video games (Phau & Liang, 2012), sometimes through peer-to-peer exchange (Allen et al., 2010). The corroborated hypotheses across the studies indicate the multifaceted nature of individuals' intentions and behaviors related to software piracy and digital content consumption. These cumulative findings suggest that attitudes toward software piracy positively influence individuals' intentions to engage in such activities (Aleassa et al., 2011; Al-Rafee & Dashti, 2012). Subjective norms, reflecting social influences, are also identified as a significant factor, positively linking to the intention to pirate software (Allen et al., 2010). The interplay between subjective norms and intention is further nuanced by the moderating role of individual traits, such as low self-control and high public self-consciousness (Aleassa et al., 2011). Ethical ideology emerges as a moderator shaping the relationship between attitude and intention to pirate software. Additionally, when examining media downloading behaviors over P2P networks, the collective impact of attitude, subjective norms, perceived behavioral control, and psychological reactance is highlighted, collectively accounting for a significant amount of variance in both intent and behavior after controlling for age and gender (e.g., Aleassa et al., 2011; Allen et al., 2010). Across different contexts, the positive associations between favorable attitudes and intentions to pirate digital material are consistent, while perceived benefits, subjective knowledge, and past piracy occurrences contribute to this intention (Phau & Liang, 2012; Plowman & Goode, 2009; Yoon, 2011). Furthermore, moral judgments on software piracy, influenced by moral recognition, moral intensity, and moral obligation, shape individuals' software piracy intentions. In the realm of online music piracy, individual attitudes, subjective norms, and perceived behavioral control play pivotal roles, with perceived risks and moral obligations influencing attitudes and intentions (Aleassa et al., 2011; Chan et al., 2013; Liao et al., 2010). The findings also shed light on the influence of justice, perceived benefits, and habit on attitudes and behavioral intentions related to digital piracy. The uncorroborated hypotheses in the domain of software piracy shed light on the intricate interplay of various factors influencing attitudes and intentions. Among these, the proposed moderating role of religiosity in the relationship between attitude and intention to pirate software remains unsupported (Aleassa et al., 2011). Similarly, when age and gender are controlled, the anticipated partial mediation of the relationships between perceived behavioral control, psychological reactance, and behavior by intent is not validated (Allen et al., 2010). The alignment of higher subjective norms with a greater intention to pirate digital material lacks empirical support (Al-Rafee & Dashti, 2012). Additionally, the negative impact of moral intensity on favorable attitudes toward piracy and the influence of perceived technical risk on the same attitudes are not substantiated (Chan et al., 2013). Contrary to expectations, subjective norms do not positively affect the intention to use pirated software. Several perceived risks, including social, prosecution, and performance, do not exhibit the expected negative effects on attitudes and intentions toward using pirated software (Liao et al., 2010). The anticipated stronger negative effect of perceived punishment certainty on attitudes toward online music piracy for females compared to males is not borne out (Morton & Koufteros, 2008). Furthermore, the hypothesized positive relationships between facilitating conditions and attitudes toward music piracy, habitual conduct and attitudes toward downloading pirated games, and social factors, facilitating conditions, and attitudes toward downloading pirated games are not supported (Nandedkar & Midha, 2012). The moderating effects of internet usage, time spent, and speed on the relationship between attitudes and intentions toward downloading pirated games are not validated (Phau & Liang, 2012). Finally, the lack of a perceived equitable relationship with music copyright owners and the perceived low quality of online music do not demonstrate the expected influences on individuals' behavioral intentions to download music from the internet (Plowman & Goode, 2009).

Others form of cybercrime investigated. Eventually, this miscellaneous category grouped a small but heterogenous set of studies. Five out of six formulated seven hypotheses that have been all corroborated. Fischer et al. (2013) found that individuals who reported being victims of scams, as opposed to those who were not victimized, demonstrated a higher likelihood of endorsing statements aligning with increased susceptibility to four psychological processes: (1) decline in decision quality in situations of heightened motivation, (2) excessive reliance on cues, (3) susceptibility to social influence techniques, and (4) responsiveness to cues related to scarcity and urgency. Kaakinen et al. (2018) found that experiencing cybercrime victimization was negatively associated with individuals' subjective well-being. This negative impact was tempered by social belongingness to offline primary groups, as such connections serve as a buffer against the adverse effects of cybercrime on well-being. Additionally, the mitigating influence extends to online communities, suggesting that a sense of belonging in virtual spaces can also alleviate the negative association between cybercrime experiences and subjective well-being. Concerning online sex offender, Middleton et al. (Middleton et al., 2009) found that in the short term, treatment could be effective in inducing positive alterations in offenders' socio-affective functioning and pro-offending attitudes. Concerning cybergrooming, Schoeps et al. (2020) discovered a positive association between body self-esteem and disinhibition with both sexting and Sexual Assertiveness Scale (SAS), with a stronger link observed for disinhibition. Furthermore, erotic sexting exhibits a stronger association with direct SAS, while pornographic sexting is more closely related to coercive SAS. Additionally, the impact of erotic-sexual variables on grooming is affirmed, with direct SAS and erotic sexting expected to exert a more substantial influence on this aspect. Eventually, Piazza and Guler (2021) found that, through a survey of over 6000 individuals in 6 Arab countries, those who actively engage with the internet for political news consumption or expressing their political views were more likely to express support for ISIS than those who followed traditional media and who engage in conventional political activity.

Conclusion: The Strain of Measuring Cybercrime in the Information Age

In this chapter, an excerpt of state of the art of the academic literature on cybercrime is presented, covering systematic reviews that have been published in academic journals in the period 2011–2021. As observed, various disciplines have shown interest in diverse dimensions of cybercrime. Concerning cyber behaviors, two primary areas of focus can be identified. The first pertains to cyberviolence, with numerous studies concentrating on phenomena such as cyberbullying, cyber harassment, and, to a lesser extent, online sexual deviance (grooming and consumption of child pornography materials). Research in these domains predominantly seeks to understand how the more typical forms of violence, extensively studied and documented in literature within physical settings, have manifested and evolved in the online realm.

The second area of interest encompasses behaviors and offenses perceived as newer and traditionally less studied due to their widespread development which was facilitated by the advent of the internet. Specifically, this includes digital piracy and a distinct form of online fraud known as phishing. In this regard, researchers have directed their attention toward explaining the origins of these behaviors, often avoiding explicit references to the previous offline context. Publications in this domain are predominantly found in journals oriented toward computer and security studies.

The vast majority of academic manuscripts generate their own data for analysis, primarily through surveys. This has translated into a multitude of studies, predominantly featuring limited population samples, with diminished external validity in terms of result generalizability. Additionally, there is observable variability in the operationalization of identical concepts, posing challenges to comparability and occasionally indicating limitations in internal validity.

An essential aspect to underscore is the non-utilization of official statistics in analyzing cybercrime. This observation is unsurprising, given that it is a relatively novel phenomenon with weak detection by official statistics. However, the weakness in official statistics remains a point to monitor in the coming years. It would be of particular interest to observe how, to what extent, and in what terms official police statistics (as well as those of convicts and the incarcerated population) may evolve into a valuable data source for research and understanding of these phenomena in the years to come.

The academic discourse today seems to be much more aware of the impossibility of subsuming under the single label of cybercrime all deviant behaviors that occur in cyberspace. Similarly, there appears to be a more widely shared opinion that different theories are needed to explain deviant behaviors online. However, a strong demand for numbers on cybercrime persists from the public opinion and policymakers. This strain is particularly pronounced in our contemporary society, which considers information and data generation as fundamental pillars of its functioning.

This chapter has shown, on one hand, how the statistical system on cybercrime is still in its early stages, and on the other hand, scientific knowledge about online deviance still requires significant research investment for a better understanding of these phenomena. However, it is important not to dismiss all the efforts that various statistical systems and the entire criminal justice system are making to meet the present and future challenges of statistical measurement. At the same time, it should not be forgotten that in recent years, the number of publications and empirical studies on cybercrime has increased significantly. Many of these studies were not included in this book because they were not cited in the systematic reviews considered. Therefore, this work acknowledges this significant limitation, likely underestimating the contribution criminologists are making to the study of cybercrime.

References

Aebi, M. F., Akdeniz, G., Barclay, G., Campistol, C., Caneppele, S., Gruszczynska, B., Harrendorf, S., Heiskanen, M., Hysi, V., Jehle, J., Jokinen, A., Kensey, A., Killias, M., Lewis, C. G., Savona, E., Smit, P., & Borisdottir, R. (2014). *European Sourcebook of Crime and Criminal Justice Statistics 2014*. European Institute for Crime Prevention and Control, affiliated with the United Nations (HEUNI).

Aebi, M. F., Caneppele, S., & Molnar, L. (2022). *Measuring cybercrime in Europe: The role of crime statistics and victimisation surveys* (Eleven). https://www.elevenpub.com/en/product/100-12642_Measuring-cybercrime-in-Europe-The-role-of-crime-statistics-and-victimisation-surveys

Ahlgrim, B., & Terrance, C. (2021). Perceptions of cyberstalking: Impact of perpetrator gender and cyberstalker/victim relationship. *Journal of Interpersonal Violence, 36*(7–8), NP4074-NP4093. https://doi.org/10.1177/0886260518784590

Ahmad, R., & Thurasamy, R. (2022). A systematic literature review of routine activity theory's applicability in cybercrimes. *Journal of Cyber Security and Mobility*, 405–432. https://doi.org/10.13052/jcsm2245-1439.1133

Ajzen, I. (1985). From intentions to actions: A theory of planned behavior. In I. J. Kuhl & J. Beckmann (Eds.), *Action control: From cognition to behavior* (pp. 11–39). Springer. https://doi.org/10.1007/978-3-642-69746-3_2

Ajzen, I., & Fishbein, M. (1980). *Understanding attitudes and predicting social behavior*. Prentice-Hall.

Akers, R. L. (1973). *Deviant behavior; a social learning approach*. Wadsworth Pub. Co.. http://archive.org/details/deviantbehaviors00aker

Aleassa, H., Pearson, J. M., & McClurg, S. (2011). Investigating software piracy in Jordan: An extension of the theory of reasoned action. *Journal of Business Ethics, 98*(4), 663–676.

Allen, P., Shepherd, K., & Roberts, L. (2010). Peer-to-peer file-sharing: Psychological reactance and the theory of planned behaviour. *International Journal of Technoethics (IJT), 1*(4), 49–64. https://doi.org/10.4018/jte.2010100104

Al-Rafee, S., & Dashti, A. E. (2012). A cross cultural comparison of the extended TPB: The case of digital piracy. *Journal of Global Information Technology Management, 15*(1), 5–24. https://doi.org/10.1080/1097198X.2012.10845610

Alsawalqa, R. O. (2021). Cyberbullying, social stigma, and self-esteem: The impact of COVID-19 on students from East and Southeast Asia at the University of Jordan. *Heliyon, 7*(4), e06711. https://doi.org/10.1016/j.heliyon.2021.e06711

Aslan, D., & Edelmann, R. (2014). Demographic and offence characteristics: A comparison of sex offenders convicted of possessing indecent images of children, committing contact sex offences or both offences. *The Journal of Forensic Psychiatry & Psychology, 25*(2), 121–134. https://doi.org/10.1080/14789949.2014.884618

Baker, E. M., Tedesco, J. C., & Baker, W. H. (2008). Consumer privacy and trust online: An experimental analysis of anti-phishing promotional effects. *Journal of Website Promotion.* https://doi.org/10.1080/15533610802104166

Bauman, S., & Pero, H. (2011). Bullying and cyberbullying among deaf students and their hearing peers: An exploratory study. *The Journal of Deaf Studies and Deaf Education, 16*(2), 236–253. https://doi.org/10.1093/deafed/enq043

Beran, T., & Li, Q. (2007). The relationship between cyberbullying and school bullying. *Journal of Student Wellbeing*, 15–33.

Caneppele, S., & Aebi, M. F. (2019). Crime drop or police recording flop? On the relationship between the decrease of offline crime and the increase of online and hybrid crimes. *Policing: A Journal of Policy and Practice, 13*(1), 66–79.

Cavezza, C., & McEwan, T. E. (2014). Cyberstalking versus off-line stalking in a forensic sample. *Psychology, Crime & Law, 20*(10), 955–970. https://doi.org/10.1080/1068316X.2014.893334

Chan, R. Y. K., Ma, K. H. Y., & Wong, Y. H. (2013). The software piracy decision-making process of Chinese computer users. *The Information Society, 29*(4), 203–218. https://doi.org/10.1080/01972243.2013.792302

Clevenger, S. L., Navarro, J. N., & Jasinski, J. L. (2016). A matter of low self-control? Exploring differences between child pornography possessors and child pornography producers/distributors using self-control theory. *Sexual Abuse, 28*(6), 555–571. https://doi.org/10.1177/1079063214557173

Cochran, J. K., Wood, P. B., Sellers, C. S., Wilkerson, W., & Chamlin, M. B. (1998). Academic dishonesty and low self-control: An empirical test of a general theory of crime. *Deviant Behavior, 19*(3), 227–255. https://doi.org/10.1080/01639625.1998.9968087

Cohen, L. E., & Felson, M. (1979). Social change and crime rate trends: A routine activity approach. *American Sociological Review, 44*(4), 588. https://doi.org/10.2307/2094589

Cornish, D. B., & Clarke, R. V. (1986). *The reasoning criminal: Rational choice perspectives on offending.* Transaction Publishers.

Cronan, T. P., & Al-Rafee, S. (2008). Factors that influence the intention to pirate software and media. *Journal of Business Ethics, 78*(4), 527–545.

Dreßing, H., Bailer, J., Anders, A., Wagner, H., & Gallas, C. (2014). Cyberstalking in a large sample of social network users: Prevalence, characteristics, and impact upon victims. *Cyberpsychology, Behavior, and Social Networking, 17*(2), 61–67. https://doi.org/10.1089/cyber.2012.0231

Eck, J. E., & Madensen, T. D. (2015). Meaningfully and artfully reinterpreting crime for useful science: An essay on the value of building with simple theory. In I. M. A. Andresen & G. Farrell (Eds.), *The criminal act: The role and influence of routine activity theory* (pp. 5–18). Palgrave Macmillan UK. https://doi.org/10.1057/9781137391322_2

Eke, A. W., Seto, M. C., & Williams, J. (2011). Examining the criminal history and future offending of child pornography offenders: An extended prospective follow-up study. *Law and Human Behavior, 35*(6), 466–478. https://doi.org/10.1007/s10979-010-9252-2

Elliott, I. A., Beech, A. R., Mandeville-Norden, R., & Hayes, E. (2009). Psychological profiles of Internet sexual offenders: Comparisons with contact sexual offenders. *Sexual Abuse, 21*(1), 76–92. https://doi.org/10.1177/1079063208326929

Federal Statistical Office. (2023, février 16). *Digital crime.* https://www.bfs.admin.ch/bfs/en/home/statistiken/kriminalitaet-strafrecht/polizei/digitale-kriminalitaet.html

Feinstein, B. A., Bhatia, V., & Davila, J. (2014). Rumination mediated the association between cyber-victimization and depressive symptoms. *Journal of Interpersonal Violence, 29*(9), 1732–1746. https://doi.org/10.1177/0886260513511534

Fischer, P., Lea, S. E. G., & Evans, K. M. (2013). Why do individuals respond to fraudulent scam communications and lose money? The psychological determinants of scam compliance. *Journal of Applied Social Psychology, 43*(10), 2060–2072. https://doi.org/10.1111/jasp.12158

Fissel, E. R., Fisher, B. S., & Nedelec, J. L. (2021). Cyberstalking perpetration among young adults: An assessment of the effects of low self-control and moral disengagement. *Crime & Delinquency, 67*(12), 1935–1961. https://doi.org/10.1177/0011128721989079

Frei, A., Erenay, N., Dittmann, V., & Graf, M. (2005). Paedophilia on the Internet—A study of 33 convicted offenders in the Canton of Lucerne. *Swiss Medical Weekly, 135*(33–34), 488–494. https://doi.org/10.4414/smw.2005.11095

Gordon, S., & Ford, R. (2006). On the definition and classification of cybercrime. *Journal in Computer Virology, 2*(1), 13–20. https://doi.org/10.1007/s11416-006-0015-z

Gottfredson, M. R., & Hirschi, T. (1990). *A general theory of crime.* Stanford University Press.

Harrison, B., Svetieva, E., & Vishwanath, A. (2016). Individual processing of phishing emails: How attention and elaboration protect against phishing. *Online Information Review, 40*(2), 265–281. https://doi.org/10.1108/OIR-04-2015-0106

Heiman, T., Olenik-Shemesh, D., & Eden, S. (2015). Cyberbullying involvement among students with ADHD: Relation to loneliness, self-efficacy and social support. *European Journal of Special Needs Education, 30*(1), 15–29. https://doi.org/10.1080/08856257.2014.943562

Hindelang, M. J., Gottfredson, M. R., & Garofalo, J. (1978). *Victims of personal crime: An empirical foundation for a theory of personal victimization.* Ballinger.

Hirschi, T. (1969). *Causes of Delinquency.* University of California Press.

Holfeld, B., & Leadbeater, B. J. (2015). The nature and frequency of cyber bullying behaviors and victimization experiences in young Canadian children. *Canadian Journal of School Psychology, 30*(2), 116–135. https://doi.org/10.1177/0829573514556853

Jung, S., & Stein, S. (2012). An examination of judicial sentencing decisions in child pornography and child molestation cases in Canada. *Journal of Criminal Psychology, 2*(1), 38–50. https://doi.org/10.1108/20093821211210486

Kaakinen, M., Keipi, T., Räsänen, P., & Oksanen, A. (2018). Cybercrime victimization and subjective well-being: An examination of the buffering effect hypothesis among adolescents and young adults. *Cyberpsychology, Behavior, and Social Networking, 21*(2), 129–137. https://doi.org/10.1089/cyber.2016.0728

Kircaburun, K., Jonason, P. K., & Griffiths, M. D. (2018). The Dark Tetrad traits and problematic social media use: The mediating role of cyberbullying and cyberstalking. *Personality and Individual Differences, 135*, 264–269. https://doi.org/10.1016/j.paid.2018.07.034

Kubiszewski, V., Fontaine, R., Potard, C., & Auzoult, L. (2015). Does cyberbullying overlap with school bullying when taking modality of involvement into account? *Computers in Human Behavior, 43*, 49–57. https://doi.org/10.1016/j.chb.2014.10.049

LaCaille, L. (2013). Theory of reasoned action. In M. D. Gellman & J. R. Turner (Éds.), *Encyclopedia of behavioral medicine* (p. 1964-1967). Springer. https://doi.org/10.1007/978-1-4419-1005-9_1619

Li, Q. (2010). Cyberbullying in high schools: A study of students' behaviors and beliefs about this new phenomenon. *Journal of Aggression, Maltreatment & Trauma, 19*(4), 372–392. https://doi.org/10.1080/10926771003788979

Liao, C., Lin, H.-N., & Liu, Y.-P. (2010). Predicting the use of pirated software: A contingency model integrating perceived risk with the theory of planned behavior. *Journal of Business Ethics, 91*(2), 237–252. https://doi.org/10.1007/s10551-009-0081-5

Long, M. L., Alison, L. A., & McManus, M. A. (2013). Child pornography and likelihood of contact abuse: A comparison between contact child sexual offenders and noncontact offenders. *Sexual Abuse, 25*(4), 370–395. https://doi.org/10.1177/1079063212464398

Low, S., & Espelage, D. (2013). *Differentiating cyber bullying perpetration from non-physical bullying: Commonalities across race, individual, and family predictors.* https://doi.org/10.1037/A0030308

Luo, X. (Robert), Zhang, W., Burd, S., & Seazzu, A. (2013). Investigating phishing victimization with the Heuristic–Systematic Model: A theoretical framework and an exploration. *Computers & Security, 38*, 28-38. https://doi.org/10.1016/j.cose.2012.12.003

McGuire, M. (2019). It ain't what it is, it's the way that they do it ? Why we still don't understand cybercrime. In *The human factor of cybercrime* (1st ed., pp. 3–28). Routledge.

Middleton, D., Mandeville-Norden, R., & Hayes, E. (2009). Does treatment work with internet sex offenders? Emerging findings from the Internet Sex Offender Treatment Programme (i-SOTP). *Journal of Sexual Aggression, 15*(1), 5–19. https://doi.org/10.1080/13552600802673444

Moneva, A., & Caneppele, S. (2020). 100% sure bets? Exploring the precipitation-control strategies of fixed-match informing websites and the environmental features of their networks. *Crime, Law and Social Change, 74*(1), 115–133. https://doi.org/10.1007/s10611-019-09871-4

Morton, N. A., & Koufteros, X. (2008). Intention to commit online music piracy and its antecedents: An empirical investigation. *Structural Equation Modeling: A Multidisciplinary Journal, 15*(3), 491–512. https://doi.org/10.1080/10705510802154331

Nandedkar, A., & Midha, V. (2012). It won't happen to me: An assessment of optimism bias in music piracy. *Computers in Human Behavior, 28*(1), 41–48. https://doi.org/10.1016/j.chb.2011.08.009

National Academies of Sciences, Engineering, and Medicine. (2018). *Modernizing crime statistics: Report 2: New systems for measuring crime.* The National Academies Press. https://doi.org/10.17226/25035

Navarro, J. N., & Jasinski, J. L. (2013). Why girls? Using routine activities theory to predict cyberbullying experiences between girls and boys. *Women & Criminal Justice, 23*(4), 286–303. https://doi.org/10.1080/08974454.2013.784225

Olweus, D. (1993). *Bullying at school: What we know and what we can do.* Blackwell.

Phau, I., & Liang, J. (2012). Downloading digital video games: Predictors, moderators and consequences. *Marketing Intelligence & Planning, 30*(7), 740–756. https://doi.org/10.1108/02634501211273832

Phillips, K., Davidson, J. C., Farr, R. R., Burkhardt, C., Caneppele, S., & Aiken, M. P. (2022). Conceptualizing cybercrime: Definitions, typologies and taxonomies. *Forensic Sciences, 2*(2), Article 2. https://doi.org/10.3390/forensicsci2020028

Piazza, J. A., & Guler, A. (2021). The online caliphate: Internet usage and ISIS support in the Arab world. *Terrorism and Political Violence, 33*(6), 1256–1275. https://doi.org/10.1080/09546553.2019.1606801

Plowman, S., & Goode, S. (2009). Factors affecting the intention to download music: Quality perceptions and downloading intensity. *Journal of Computer Information Systems, 15*.

Pratt, T. C., & Turanovic, J. J. (2014). General theory of crime. In I. G. Bruinsma & D. Weisburd (Eds.), *Encyclopedia of criminology and criminal justice* (pp. 1900–1907). Springer. https://doi.org/10.1007/978-1-4614-5690-2_357

Price, M., Chin, M. A., Higa-McMillan, C., Kim, S., & Christopher Frueh, B. (2013). Prevalence and internalizing problems of ethnoracially diverse victims of traditional and cyber bullying. *School Mental Health, 5*(4), 183–191. https://doi.org/10.1007/s12310-013-9104-6

Ratcliffe, J. H. (2008). *Intelligence-led policing.* Willan Publishing. https://doi.org/10.4324/9780203118245

Reyns, B. W. (2019). Online pursuit in the twilight zone: Cyberstalking perpetration by college students. *Victims & Offenders, 14*(2), 183–198. https://doi.org/10.1080/15564886.2018.1557092

Reyns, B. W., Fisher, B. S., & Randa, R. (2018). Explaining cyberstalking victimization against college women using a multitheoretical approach: Self-control, opportunity, and control balance. *Crime & Delinquency, 64*(13), 1742–1764. https://doi.org/10.1177/0011128717753116

Robert K. Merton. (1968). *Robert K. Merton—Social Theory and Social Structure*. http://archive. org/details/robert_k_merton_social_theory_and_social_structure

Schoeps, K., Peris Hernández, M., Garaigordobil, M., & Montoya-Castilla, I. (2020). Risk factors for being a victim of online grooming in adolescents. *Psicothema, 32*(1), 15–23. https://doi.org/10.7334/psicothema2019.179

Seiler, S. J., & Navarro, J. N. (2014). Bullying on the pixel playground: Investigating risk factors of cyberbullying at the intersection of children's online-offline social lives. *Cyberpsychology: Journal of Psychosocial Research on Cyberspace, 8*(4), Article 4. https://doi.org/10.5817/CP2014-4-6

Seto, M. C., Cantor, J. M., & Blanchard, R. (2006). Child pornography offenses are a valid diagnostic indicator of pedophilia. *Journal of Abnormal Psychology, 115*(3), 610–615. https://doi.org/10.1037/0021-843X.115.3.610

Seto, M. C., Reeves, L., & Jung, S. (2010). Explanations given by child pornography offenders for their crimes. *Journal of Sexual Aggression, 16*(2), 169–180. https://doi.org/10.1080/13552600903572396

Seto, M. C., Wood, J. M., Babchishin, K. M., & Flynn, S. (2012). Online solicitation offenders are different from child pornography offenders and lower risk contact sexual offenders. *Law and Human Behavior, 36*(4), 320–330. https://doi.org/10.1037/h0093925

Sutherland, E. H. (1940). White-collar criminality. *American Sociological Review, 5*(1), 1–12. JSTOR. https://doi.org/10.2307/2083937

Tsakalidis, G., & Vergidis, K. (2019). A systematic approach toward description and classification of cybercrime incidents. *IEEE Transactions on Systems, Man, and Cybernetics: Systems, 49*(4), 710–729. https://doi.org/10.1109/TSMC.2017.2700495

UK Statistics Authority. (2014). Assessment of compliance with the code of practice for official statistics: statistics on crime in England and Wales. *Assessment Report 268*.

van Duyne, P. C. (2006). Introduction: Counting clouds and measuring organised crime. In *The organisation of crime for profit: Conduct, law and measurement* (pp. 1–16). Wolf Legal Publishers (WLP).

Vishwanath, A., Herath, T., Chen, R., Wang, J., & Rao, H. R. (2011). Why do people get phished? Testing individual differences in phishing vulnerability within an integrated, information processing model. *Decision Support Systems, 51*(3), 576–586. https://doi.org/10.1016/j.dss.2011.03.002

Wall, D. S. (2001). Cybercrime and the internet. In *Crime and the Internet* (pp. 1–17). Routledge.

Wall, D. (2007). *Cybercrime: The transformation of crime in the information age*. Polity Press.

Wall, D. S. (2015). The internet as a conduit for criminal activity. In *Information technology and the criminal justice system* (pp. 77–98). SAGE Publications, Inc.. https://papers.ssrn.com/abstract=740626

Workman, M. (2008). Wisecrackers: A theory-grounded investigation of phishing and pretext social engineering threats to information security. *Journal of the American Society for Information Science and Technology, 59*(4), 662–674. https://doi.org/10.1002/asi.20779

Wright, R., & Marett, K. (2010). The influence of experiential and dispositional factors in phishing: An empirical investigation of the deceived. *Journal of Management Information Systems, 27*(1), 273–303. https://doi.org/10.2753/MIS0742-1222270111

Yar, M. (2005). The novelty of 'cybercrime': An assessment in light of routine activity theory. *European Journal of Criminology, 2*(4), 407–427. https://doi.org/10.1177/147737080556056

Yoon, C. (2011). Theory of planned behavior and ethics theory in digital piracy: An integrated model. *Journal of Business Ethics, 100*(3), 405–417. https://doi.org/10.1007/s10551-010-0687-7

Zalaquett, C. P., & Chatters, S. J. (2014). Cyberbullying in college: Frequency, characteristics, and practical implications. *SAGE Open, 4*(1), 2158244014526721. https://doi.org/10.1177/2158244014526721

Open Access This chapter is licensed under the terms of the Creative Commons Attribution 4.0 International License (http://creativecommons.org/licenses/by/4.0/), which permits use, sharing, adaptation, distribution and reproduction in any medium or format, as long as you give appropriate credit to the original author(s) and the source, provide a link to the Creative Commons license and indicate if changes were made.

The images or other third party material in this chapter are included in the chapter's Creative Commons license, unless indicated otherwise in a credit line to the material. If material is not included in the chapter's Creative Commons license and your intended use is not permitted by statutory regulation or exceeds the permitted use, you will need to obtain permission directly from the copyright holder.

Epilogue: The Evolution of Crime in Our Hybrid Society: Looking Back, Looking Forward, and Looking More Carefully

As explored throughout this volume, the relationship between digitalization and crime trends is more complex and nuanced than initially understood. Through five interconnected chapters, this book has traced the theoretical foundations, empirical evidence, and methodological challenges in understanding crime in our hybrid society, where physical and digital spaces increasingly overlap and influence each other.

The progression of chapters has revealed several insights. First, we have seen how criminology's progressive ethos, rooted in Enlightenment principles, shapes our approach to understanding technological change and crime. This historical perspective, explored in Chap. 1, helps explain both the achievements and limitations of criminological responses to digital transformation.

Second, the examination of the "international crime drop" debate in Chap. 2 has shown that what appeared to be a universal decline in crime was actually a more complex phenomenon, with significant variations across different types of offenses, regions, and time periods. This analysis highlighted the importance of considering both offline and online criminal activities when assessing crime trends.

Third, through the theoretical exploration presented in Chap. 3, we have developed a more sophisticated understanding of how digitalization influences social change and crime patterns. The chapter's proposed conjecture about the mechanisms linking digital transformation to criminal behavior provides a framework for understanding both direct and indirect effects of technological change on crime opportunities.

Fourth, the empirical investigation of the "digital leisure hypothesis" in Chap. 4 has provided concrete evidence for how digital entertainment, particularly among youth, has contributed to shifting patterns of criminal opportunity. The chapter's analysis of pre- and post-COVID-19 data has further showed how accelerated digitalization affects crime patterns.

Finally, the systematic review of cybercrime research in Chap. 5 has revealed a series of methodological challenges and opportunities in studying crime in the digital age. This analysis has highlighted both the progress made in understanding various forms of cybercrime and the significant gaps that remain in our ability to measure and analyze these phenomena effectively.

Several key conclusions emerge from this book:

1. The impact of digitalization on crime cannot be reduced to a simple displacement from physical to digital spaces. Instead, we have witnessed a fundamental transformation in how criminal opportunities arise and are exploited in our hybrid society.
2. Changes in routine activities, particularly among young people, have played a crucial role in shifting crime patterns. The increasing time spent in digital environments has not only reduced opportunities for certain types of traditional crime but has also created new opportunities for online offending.
3. Traditional criminological theories, particularly those focused on opportunity structures, remain relevant but must be adapted to account for the unique characteristics of digital and hybrid criminal environments.
4. The COVID-19 pandemic has accelerated preexisting trends toward digitalization, offering a natural experiment that supports many of our theoretical predictions about the relationship between digital activity and crime patterns.
5. Current methods for measuring cybercrime face significant limitations, from definitional challenges to data collection issues, highlighting the need for more sophisticated research approaches.

Looking ahead, several challenges and opportunities warrant attention:

- The need for better measurement tools and methodologies to capture crime in hybrid environments
- The importance of understanding how emerging technologies might further transform criminal opportunities
- The challenge of developing effective prevention strategies that work across both physical and digital domains
- The necessity of adapting law enforcement and criminal justice responses to hybrid forms of crime
- The critical need to improve official statistics and research methodologies to better capture online and hybrid crimes

As we move further into the digital age, the insights presented in this volume remind us that criminology must continue to evolve, developing new theoretical frameworks and methodological approaches that can capture the increasingly hybrid nature of criminal behavior. This evolution must occur not only in how we theorize about crime but also in how we measure and study it.

This work represents a step toward that understanding, but much remains to be explored. The transformation of our society through digitalization continues, and with it, the patterns and possibilities of criminal behavior will continue to evolve. Future research can build on these foundations to develop even more sophisticated methods for understanding and measuring crime in our hybrid world.

Lausanne, Switzerland	Marcelo F. Aebi
Elche, Spain	Fernando Miró-Llinares
Lausanne, Switzerland	Stefano Caneppele
January 2025	

Index

C
Comparative criminology, 24, 31
COVID-19 lockdowns, 51, 77–80, 83, 96
Crime measurement, 31
Crime opportunities, 38, 57, 61, 79, 81, 83, 86, 88, 90, 93–96
Criminal opportunities, 25–27, 30, 31, 46, 47, 49, 51, 59, 60, 68, 79–82, 84, 85, 93, 94, 96, 106
Criminological theories, 8–11, 13, 23, 24, 31, 39, 54, 105, 108, 109, 112–114
Cybercrime, 18, 19, 23, 30, 31, 39, 40, 47, 48, 53, 58–63, 68, 78, 80, 82–84, 86, 95, 96, 101–123
Cybercrime research, 101–123

D
Digital leisure, 53, 56, 57, 60, 80, 88–93
Digital transformation, 80, 96

E
Enlightenment, 2–8, 13

G
Global trend, 59

I
Interdisciplinary approaches, 109
International crime drop, 17–40

M
Measurement challenges, 102–105, 108, 123
Methodological challenges, 39
Methodological rigor, 33
Multifaceted model, 83

O
Offline crime, 11–13, 18, 24, 27, 30, 32, 36, 38, 46, 47, 51–69, 112
Online gaming, 80, 88, 90
Online offenses, 18

P
Policy implications, 40
Problem-solving, 3, 6, 7, 10, 13
Progressive ethos, 1–13

R
Reform-oriented, 3, 5, 7, 10, 12, 13
Research methodologies, 31
Routine activities, 9, 25, 27, 30, 31, 36, 38, 52–54, 63, 66, 68, 69, 78

S
Security measures, 24, 26, 27, 40
Social interactions, 66
Systematic reviews, 101–123

T
Technological changes, 39, 40, 48–51, 53, 54, 63
Theoretical frameworks, 115